Mike McGrath

Visual Basic

4th edition
covers Visual Studio Community 2015

In easy steps is an imprint of In Easy Steps Limited
16 Hamilton Terrace · Holly Walk · Leamington Spa
Warwickshire · United Kingdom · CV32 4LY
www.ineasysteps.com

Fourth Edition

Notice of Liability
Every effort has been made to ensure that this book contains accurate
and current information. However, In Easy Steps Limited and the
author shall not be liable for any loss or damage suffered by readers
as a result of any information contained herein.

Trademarks
All trademarks are acknowledged as belonging to their respective
companies.

In Easy Steps Limited supports The Forest Stewardship Council (FSC),
the leading international forest certification organization. All our titles
that are printed on Greenpeace approved FSC certified paper carry the
FSC logo.

MIX
Paper from
responsible sources
FSC® C020837

Printed and bound in the United Kingdom

ISBN 978-1-84078-701-6

Contents

4 Learning the language   55

5 Building an application   79

1 Getting started

Welcome to the exciting
world of Visual Basic
programming. This chapter
introduces the Visual Studio
Integrated Development
Environment (IDE) and
shows you how to create a
real Windows application.

Introducing Visual Basic

In choosing to start programming with Visual Basic you have made an excellent choice – the Visual Basic programming language offers the easiest way to write programs for Windows. This means you can easily create your own programs to give maximum control over your computer, and automate your work to be more productive. Also, programming with Visual Basic is fun!

Like other programming languages, Visual Basic comprises a number of significant "keywords" and a set of syntax rules. Beginners often find its syntax simpler than other programming languages, making Visual Basic a popular first choice to learn.

Although writing programs can be complex, Visual Basic makes it easy to get started. You can choose how far to go. Another advantage of Visual Basic is that it works with Microsoft Office applications, and with the Windows Script Host within the Windows operating system – so the possibilities are immense.

You can download the projects from this book at **www.ineasysteps. com/resource-centre/ downloads/**

- **Visual Basic (VB)** – quite simply the best programming language for the novice or hobbyist to begin creating their own standalone Windows applications, fast.
- **Visual Basic for Applications (VBA)** – an implementation of Visual Basic that is built into all Microsoft Office applications. It runs within a host, rather than as a standalone application.
- **Visual Basic Script (VBScript)** – a derivative of Visual Basic that can be used for Windows scripting.

The **New** icon pictured above indicates a new or enhanced feature introduced with the latest version of Visual Basic and Visual Studio.

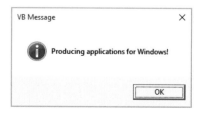

The evolution of Visual Basic

- Visual Basic 1.0 released in May 1991 at the Comdex trade show in Atlanta, Georgia, USA.
- Visual Basic 2.0 released in November 1992 – introducing an easier and faster programming environment.
- Visual Basic 3.0 released in the summer of 1993 – introducing the Microsoft Jet Database Engine for database programs.
- Visual Basic 4.0 released in August 1995 – introducing support for controls based on the Component Object Model (COM).
- Visual Basic 5.0 released in February 1997 – introducing the ability to create custom user controls.
- Visual Basic 6.0 released in the summer of 1998 – introducing the ability to create web-based programs. This hugely popular edition is the final version based on COM and is often referred to today as "Classic Visual Basic".
- Visual Basic 7.0 (also known as Visual Basic .NET) released in 2002 – introducing a very different object-oriented language based upon the Microsoft .NET framework. This controversial edition broke backward-compatibility with previous versions, causing a rift in the developer community. Subsequent editions added features for subsequent .NET framework releases.
- Visual Basic 8.0 (a.k.a. Visual Basic 2005).
- Visual Basic 9.0 (a.k.a. Visual Basic 2008).
- Visual Basic 10.0 (a.k.a. Visual Basic 2010).
- Visual Basic 11.0 (a.k.a. Visual Basic 2012).
- Visual Basic 12.0 (a.k.a. Visual Basic 2013).
  (version numbering of Visual Basic skipped 13 to keep in line with the version numbering of Visual Studio itself).
- Visual Basic 14.0 (a.k.a. Visual Basic 2015).

All examples in this book have been created for Visual Basic 14.0, although many of the core language features are common to previous versions of the Visual Basic programming language.

Visual Basic derives from an earlier, simple language called BASIC, an acronym –
Beginners
All-purpose
Symbolic
Instruction
Code.
The "Visual" part was added later as many tasks can now be accomplished visually, without actually writing any code.

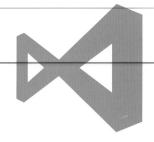

Installing Visual Studio

In order to create Windows applications with the Visual Basic programming language, you will first need to install a Visual Studio Integrated Development Environment (IDE).

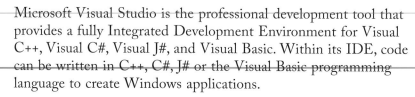

Microsoft Visual Studio is the professional development tool that provides a fully Integrated Development Environment for Visual C++, Visual C#, Visual J#, and Visual Basic. Within its IDE, code can be written in C++, C#, J# or the Visual Basic programming language to create Windows applications.

Visual Studio Community edition is a streamlined version of Visual Studio specially created for those people learning programming. It has a simplified user interface and omits advanced features of the professional edition to avoid confusion. Within its IDE, code can be written in the Visual Basic programming language to create Windows applications.

Both Visual Studio and Visual Studio Community provide a Visual Basic IDE for Visual Basic programming. Unlike the fully-featured Visual Studio product, the Visual Studio Community edition is completely free and can be installed on any system meeting the following minimum requirements:

Component	Requirement
Operating system	Windows XP Windows Vista Windows 7 Windows 8/8.1 Windows 10
CPU (processor)	1.6GHz or faster
RAM (memory)	1024MB (1GB) minimum
HDD (hard drive)	4GB available space, 5400RPM speed
Video Card	DirectX 9-capable, and a screen resolution of 1024 x 768 or higher

The Visual Studio Community edition is used throughout this book to demonstrate programming with the Visual Basic language, but the examples can also be recreated in Visual Studio. Follow the steps opposite to install Visual Studio Community edition.

...cont'd

1 Open your web browser and navigate to the Visual Studio Community download page – at the time of writing this can be found at **visual-studio.com/en-us/products/visual-studio-community-vs.aspx**

2 Click the "Download Community 2015" button to download a **vs_community.exe** installer file to your computer

3 Click on the **vs_community.exe** file to run the installer

4 Accept the suggested installation location, then click **Next**

5 Choose the **Custom** type of installation, then click **Next**

6 Check only the **Microsoft SQL Server Data Tools** feature to be added to the typical setup, then click **Next**, **Install** to begin the download and installation process

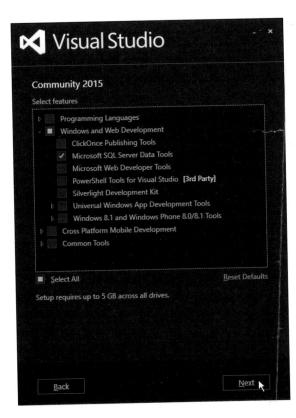

Choosing a different destination folder may require other paths to be adjusted later – it's simpler to just accept the suggested default.

The Visual Studio 2015 setup process allows you to install just the components you need.

You can run the installer again at a later date to modify Visual Studio by adding or removing features. The **Microsoft SQL Server Data Tools** are required by the database example in the final chapter of this book.

Exploring the IDE

1 Go to the Start menu, then select the Visual Studio 2015 menu item added there by the installer

Beware

The first time Visual Studio starts, it takes a few minutes as it performs some configuration routines.

Hot tip

You can change the color theme later – choose the **Tools**, **Options** menu then **Environment**, **General**.

2 Sign in with your Microsoft Account, or simply click the **Not now, maybe later** link to continue

3 Choose your preferred color theme, such as **Light**, then click the **Start Visual Studio** button

The Visual Studio Integrated Development Environment (IDE) appears, from which you have instant access to everything needed to produce complete Windows applications. From here you can create exciting visual interfaces, enter code, compile and execute applications, debug errors, and much more.

The Visual Studio IDE initially includes a default Start Page, along with the standard IDE components, and looks like this:

Menu Bar

Toolbar

Toolbox

Recent Projects

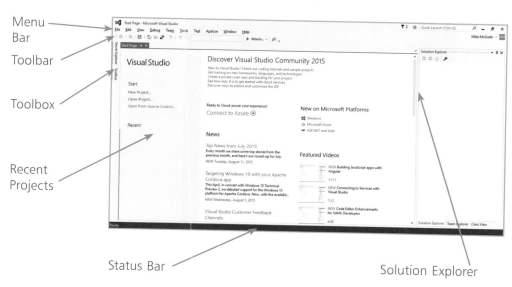

Status Bar

Solution Explorer

Start Page elements

The default start page provides these useful features:

- **Start** – provides links you can click to begin a new project or reopen an existing project.
- **Recent** – conveniently lists recently opened projects so you can quickly select one to reopen.
- **News** – feeds the latest online news direct from the Microsoft Developer Network (MSDN).

Visual Studio IDE components

The Visual Studio IDE initially provides these standard features:

- **Menu Bar** – where you can select actions to perform on all your project files and to access Help. When a project is open, extra menus of Project and Build are shown in addition to the default menu selection of File, Edit, View, Debug, Team, Tools, Test, Analyze, Window, and Help.
- **Toolbar** – where you can perform the most popular menu actions with just a single click on its associated shortcut icon.
- **Toolbox** – where you can select visual elements to add to a project. Place the cursor over the Toolbox to see its contents. When a project is open, "controls" such as Button, Label, CheckBox, RadioButton, and TextBox are shown here.
- **Solution Explorer** – where you can see at a glance all the files and resource components contained within an open project.
- **Status Bar** – where you can read the state of the current activity being undertaken. When building an application, a "Build started" message is displayed here, changing to a "Build succeeded" or "Build failed" message upon completion.

You can return to the Start Page at any time by selecting **View**, **Start Page** on the menu bar.

The menus are once again in title-case, rather than the ALL CAPS style of the previous version.

Online elements of the Start Page require a live internet connection – if the hyperlinks do not appear to work, verify your internet connection.

Starting a new project

1 On the menu bar click **File**, **New**, **Project**, or press the **Ctrl + Shift + N** keys, to open the New Project dialog box

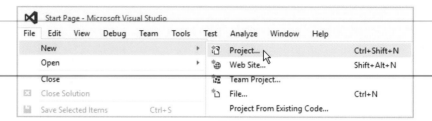

2 In the New Project dialog box, select the **Windows Forms Application** template icon

3 Enter a project name of your choice in the **Name** field, then click on the **OK** button to create the new project – in this case the project name will be "GettingStarted"

Visual Studio now creates your new project and loads it into the IDE. A new tabbed **Form Designer** window appears (in place of the Start Page tabbed window) displaying a default empty Form. You can select **View**, and then the **Solution Explorer** menu, to open a Solution Explorer window that reveals all files in your project. Additionally, you can select **View**, **Properties** menu to open a **Properties** window to reveal all properties of your Form.

The **New Project** dialog automatically selects the **Windows Forms Application** template by default as it is the most often used template.

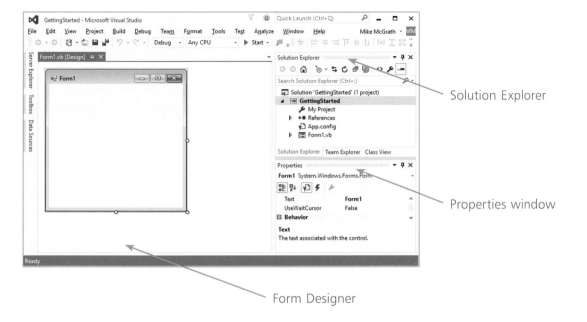

Solution Explorer

Properties window

Form Designer

The **Form Designer** is where you can create visual interfaces for your applications, and the **Properties** window contains details of the item that is currently selected in the Form Designer window.

The Visual Studio IDE has now gathered all the resources needed to build a default Windows application – click the **Start** button on the toolbar to launch this application.

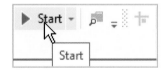

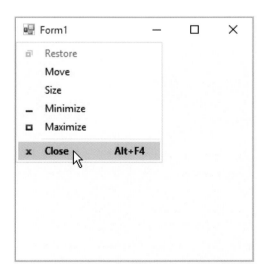

The application creates a basic window – you can move it, minimize it, maximize it, resize it, and quit the application by closing it. It may not do much but you have already created a real Windows program!

You can alternatively run applications using the **Debug**, **Start Debugging** menu options.

Adding a visual control

The **Toolbox** in the Visual Studio IDE contains a wide range of visual controls which are the building blocks of your applications. Using the project created on the previous page, follow these steps to start using the Toolbox now:

The **Toolbox** will automatically hide when you click on another part of the IDE, but it can be fixed in place so it will never hide, using the ⊞ pin button on the Toolbox bar.

1 Place the cursor over the vertical **Toolbox** tab at the left edge of the IDE window, or click **View**, **Toolbox** on the menu bar, to display the Toolbox contents. The visual controls are contained under various category headings beside an ▷ expansion arrow

2 Click on the expansion arrow beside the **Common Controls** category heading to expand the list of most commonly used visual controls. Usefully, each control name appears beside an icon depicting that control as a reminder. You can click on the category heading again to collapse the list, then expand the other categories to explore the range of controls available to build your application interfaces

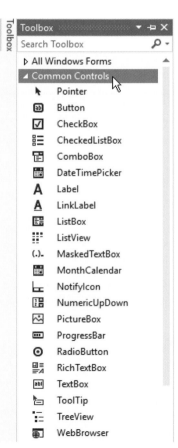

Any pinned Window in the IDE can be dragged from its usual location to any position you prefer. Drag it back to the initial location to re-dock it.

3 Click and drag the **Button** item from the Common Controls category in the Toolbox onto the Form in the Designer window, or double-click the Button item, to add a Button control to the Form

 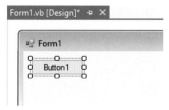

The Button control appears in the Form Designer surrounded by "handles" which can be dragged to resize the button's width and height. Click the ▶ **Start** button to run the application and try out your button.

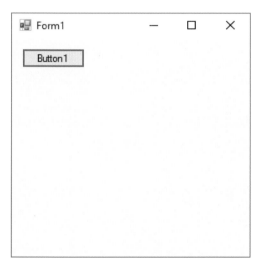

The Button control behaves in a familiar Windows application manner with "states" that visually react to the cursor.

Default State   Hover State   Down State

A **Button** is one of the most useful interface controls – your program determines what happens when the user clicks it.

This **Button** control performs no function when it's clicked – until you add some code.

17

Adding functional code

The Visual Studio IDE automatically generates code, in the background, to incorporate the visual controls you add to your program interface. Additional code can be added manually, using the IDE's integral **Code Editor**, to determine how your program should respond to interface events – such as when the user clicks a button.

Using the project created on the previous page, follow these steps to start using the Visual Studio Code Editor:

1 Double-click on the **Button** control you have added to the default Form in the Designer window. A new tabbed text window opens in the IDE – this is the **Code Editor** window

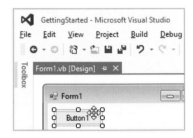

2 The cursor is automatically placed at precisely the right point in the code at which to add an instruction, to determine what the program should do when this button is clicked. Type the instruction **MsgBox("Hello World!")** so the Code Editor looks like this:

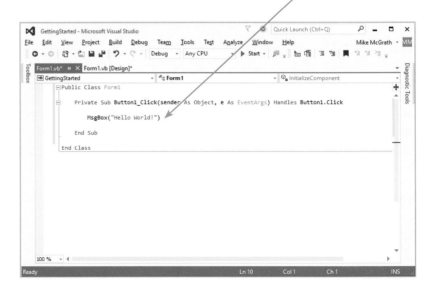

18

...cont'd

 Click the **Start** button to run the application and test the code you have just written, to handle the event that occurs when the button is clicked

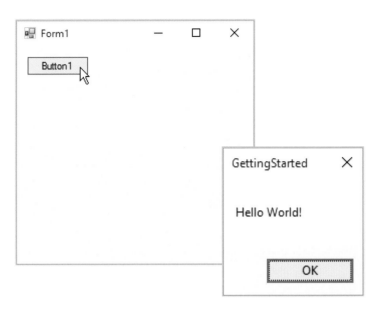

Use the **View** menu on the menu bar to open the **Code Editor**, **Form Designer**, or any other window you require at any time.

Click the **OK** button to close the dialog box, then click the **X** button on the Form window, or click the **Stop Debugging** button on the menu bar, to stop the program

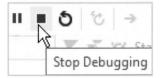

Each time the button in this application is pressed, the program reads the line of code you added manually to produce a dialog box containing the specified message. The action of pressing the button creates a **Click** event that refers to the associated "event-handler" section of code you added to see how to respond.

In fact, most Windows software works by responding to events in this way. For instance, when you press a key in a word processor a character appears in the document – the **KeyPress** event calls upon its event-handler code to update the text in response.

The process of providing intelligent responses to events in your programs is the very cornerstone of creating Windows applications with Visual Basic.

Saving projects

Even the simplest Visual Basic project comprises multiple files which must each be saved on your system to store the project.

Follow these steps to save the current New Project to disk:

You can click **File**, **Close Solution** on the menu bar to close an open project – a dialog will prompt you to save any changes before closing.

1 Click the **Save All** button on the toolbar, or click **File**, **Save All** on the menu bar, or press **Ctrl + Shift + S**

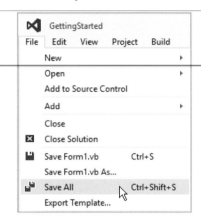

2 Your project is now saved at its default save location

3 To discover or change the save location click **Tools** on the menu bar, then select the **Options** item

4 Expand **Projects and Solutions** in the left pane, then choose the **General** option to reveal **Projects location**

Find the **Debug** folder in your saved project directory containing the application's executable (**.exe**) file – you can double-click this to run your program like other Windows applications.

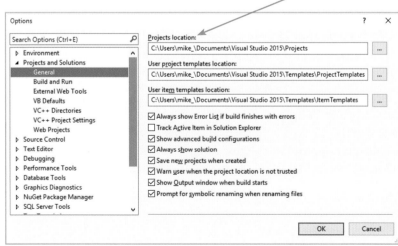

Reopening projects

Use these steps to reopen a saved Visual Basic project:

1 Click **File**, **Open**, **Project/Solution** on the menu bar to launch the **Open Project** dialog

Beware

Only have one project open at any given time to avoid confusion – unless several are needed to be opened together for advanced programming.

2 In the **Open Project** dialog, select the folder containing the project you wish to reopen, and **Open** that folder

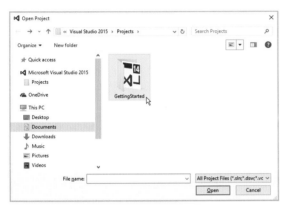

3 Now, select the Visual Basic Solution file with the extension **.sln** to reopen the project, or alternatively, open the folder bearing the project name, then select the Visual Basic Project File with the extension **.vbproj**

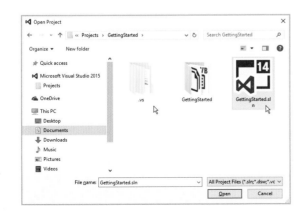

Hot tip

If you don't see the Form Designer window after you have reopened a project, click the **Form1.vb** icon in **Solution Explorer** to make it appear.

Summary

- The **Windows Application Template** in the New Project dialog is used to begin a new Windows application project.
- A unique name should be entered into the **New Project** dialog whenever you create a new Visual Basic project.
- The **Form Designer** window of the Visual Studio IDE is where you create the visual interface for your program.
- Visual controls are added from the **Toolbox** to create the interface layout you want for your program.
- A control can be dragged from the **Toolbox** and dropped onto the Form, or added to the Form with a double-click.
- The **Visual Studio IDE** automatically generates code in the background as you develop your program visually.
- The **Code Editor** window of the Visual Studio IDE is where you manually add extra code to your program.
- Double-click on any control in the **Form Designer** to open the Code Editor window at that control's event-handler code.
- The **Start** button on the Visual Studio toolbar can be used to run the current project application.
- Pressing a Button control in a running application creates a **Click** event within the program.
- Code added to a button's **Click** event-handler determines how your program will respond whenever its Click event occurs.
- Providing intelligent responses to events in your programs is the cornerstone of programming with Visual Basic.
- Remember to explicitly save your working project using the **Save All** button on the toolbar, to avoid accidental loss.
- Select the solution file with the **.sln** extension in your chosen saved project directory to reopen that project.

2 Setting properties

This chapter describes how properties of an application can be changed at "designtime", when you are creating the interface, and at "runtime", when the application is actually in use.

Form properties

Most applications created with Visual Basic are based upon a windowed **Form** – a canvas on which to paint the user interface. In some cases, an application will have more than one Form, and Visual Basic lets you display and hide Forms while the application is running. Closing the main Form quits the application.

Like all Visual Basic objects, each Form has several interesting, familiar properties, such as those distinguished below:

Icon – a small graphic appearing at the top left corner of the open Form, and visible when it's minimized

Text – a caption appearing in the title bar of the open Form, and visible when it's minimized

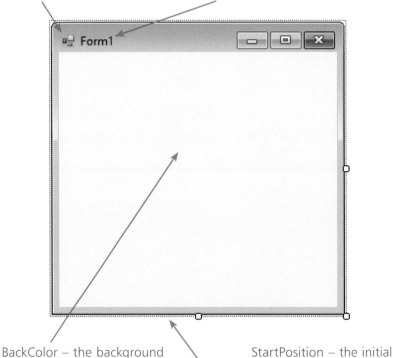

BackColor – the background color of the Form

StartPosition – the initial location of the Form on the Windows desktop

Size – the height and width of the Form

A **Form** is a window. That is why Forms have a Maximize, Minimize and Close button, like all other regular windows.

Meeting the properties editor

The Visual Studio IDE provides a **Properties** window where object properties can be inspected. This displays a list of the currently selected object's properties, and their current values. The full list of Form properties, for example, is much larger than the few shown on the previous page, and can be inspected in the property editor.

1 Identify the Properties window in the IDE – if it's not visible click **View**, **Properties Window** to open it

2 Click on **File**, **New**, **Project** to start a new **Windows Forms Application** using the suggested default name

3 Click on the blank **Form** in the Form Designer window to display its properties in the **Properties** window

4 Try out the Properties window buttons, immediately above the properties list, to explore different types of categorized and alphabetical displays

5 Use the scroll bar in the Properties window to examine the complete list of Form properties and their present values

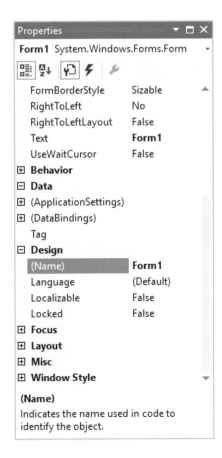

Hot tip

Every object in Visual Basic has a name – the name of the currently selected object appears in the drop-down list at the top of the **Properties** window.

Beware

Although "Form1" is the default value for both **Text** and **(Name)** properties, it is important to recognize that the Text property only sets the Form's caption, whereas the (Name) property is used to reference that Form in Visual Basic programming code.

Editing property values

Changing the properties of a Visual Basic object allows you to determine the appearance of that object. When creating an interface, at designtime, an object's **Size** property can be changed by moving its handles to resize it in the Form Designer window – its new dimension values will then appear in the Properties window. More usefully, the value of each single **Form** and **Control** property can be edited directly in the Properties window.

Editing a Form property value

1 Click on a default blank **Form** in the Form Designer window to display its properties in the Properties window

2 Find the **Text** property in the Properties window, then double-click in the value column alongside it to highlight the present value – this will be "Form1" by default

3 Type "New Caption" to specify that as a new value for the **Text** property – the text string appears in the value column as you type

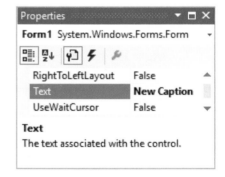

4 Hit **Enter**, or click anywhere else, to apply the new value – it now also appears on the Form in the Form Designer

Beware

Although a new value has been assigned to the Form's **Text** property, its **(Name)** property still has the default value of "Form1" for reference in Visual Basic programming code.

...cont'd

Editing a Control property value

1 Click **View**, then **Toolbox** on the menu bar or press **Ctrl + Alt + X**, to open the ToolBox

2 Click and drag the **Label** item from the **Common Controls** category, or double-click on it, to add a Label control to a blank default Form

3 In the Form Designer window, double-click on the Label control to display its present property values in the **Properties** window

4 Find the **Text** property in the Properties window, then double-click in the value column alongside it to highlight the present value – this will be "Label1" by default

5 Type "New Label Text" to specify that as a new value for the **Text** property – the text string appears in the value column as you type

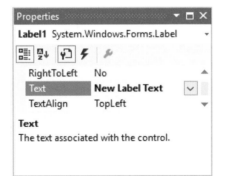

6 Hit **Enter,** or click anywhere else, to apply the new value – it now also appears on the Label in the Form Designer

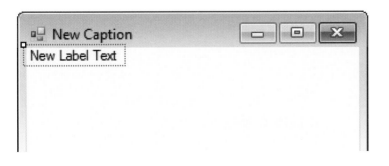

Some properties, such as **Icon**, provide a Browse button when you click on their value column, so you can navigate to the location of a local resource to select as the new property value.

Whenever you make changes in the IDE, Visual Basic works in the background to make associated changes to the underlying code.

Coding property values

In addition to setting property design values for your application in the **Properties** window, you may also set some text and color values in programming code, so the properties get assigned their initial values (they are "initialized") when the Form first loads.

Statements to initialize property values should be placed within the Form's **Load** event-handler. This executes the statements it contains when it is called by the action of the Form loading, just as the **Click** event-handler executes its statements when it is called by the action of a user clicking the **Button**.

Initializing Control properties

1 Click on **File**, **New**, **Project** to start a new **Windows Forms Application** and name it "Initialize"

2 Click and drag a **Label** item from the Toolbox's **Common Controls** category, or double-click on it, to add a Label control to a blank default Form

3 In the Form Designer window, double-click anywhere on the default Form to launch the **Code Editor** – the cursor is automatically placed in the Form's **Load** event-handler section of code, ready to add statements

The Visual Basic **Color** object lets you specify a wide range of colors. Try adding an instruction to set this label's **ForeColor** property to **Color.Red**.

4 Type the instruction **Label1.BackColor = Color.Yellow** to set the Label's background color to yellow, then hit **Enter**

5 Type the instruction **Label1.Text = "Initialized Text"** to set the Label's text content, then hit **Enter**

6 Click on the **Start** button to run the application and see that the Label properties initialize with the values you have specified

28

...cont'd

Initializing Form properties

1 Click the **Stop Debugging** button to halt the Initialize application and return once more to the **Code Editor** at the Form's **Load** event-handler section of code

2 Add the instruction **Form1.BackColor = Color.Blue** to attempt to set the Form's background to blue, then hit **Enter** – notice that a red wavy underline now appears beneath **Form1.BackColor** on this line of code

You need to hit the **Enter** key after typing each statement so that only one statement appears on each line.

3 Place the mouse pointer over the red wavy line and read the **ToolTip** message that pops up

```
Form1.BackColor = Color.Blue
```
🔧 Property My.MyProject.MyForms.Form1 As Form1

'Form1' cannot refer to itself through its default instance; use 'Me' instead.

4 The ToolTip message means you cannot refer to the Form by its name within its own event-handler, so change the instruction to **Me.BackColor = Color.Blue** – now hit **Enter** and see the red wavy underline disappear

5 Type the instruction **Me.Text = "Initialized Caption"** to set the Form's text caption, then hit **Enter**

6 Click on the **Start** button to run the application and see that the Form properties initialize with the values you have specified

Use the special **Me** keyword in place of the Form's name if you want to directly address the Form.

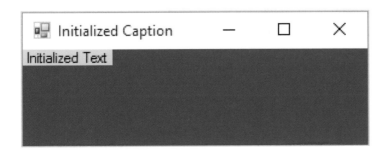

Applying computed values

The **Properties** window and initialization code technique allows the programmer to specify static property values at designtime. Creating code to calculate further values from known static values allows your application to compute property values at runtime.

Use the guidelines that appear as you drag controls around the Form, to easily align them.

1 Click on **File**, **New**, **Project** to start a new **Windows Forms Application** and name it "Compute"

2 From the ToolBox, add six **Label** controls and one **Button** control to the default Form, then drag them into position so the Form looks something like the arrangement below

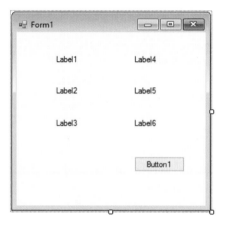

3 Selecting each item in turn, use the Properties window to change the **Text** property value of the Form, Button, and all Labels, to look like this:

4 To avoid confusion with other controls, use the Properties window to change the **(Name)** property of the three Labels down the right-hand side of the form to **Num1, Num2,** and **Sum,** reading from top-to-bottom – the new names can now be used in Visual Basic programming code to refer to these controls

5 Double-click the **Button** to open the **Code Editor** within its **Click** event-handler section of code. Here's where a statement can be added to calculate the total of the static **Text** property values of **Num1** and **Num2**

6 Type **Sum.Text = Val(Num1.Text) + Val(Num2.Text)** then hit **Enter** to add a statement assigning the computed total value to the sum Label's **Text** property

7 Click on the **Start** button to run the application. Click the button to execute the statement you added and see the **Sum** total value appear

The Visual Basic **Val()** function is used here to extract the numeric version of the text string values, so it can perform arithmetic on them – arithmetic functions are fully explained later.

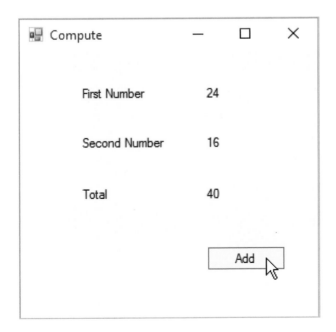

Compute	—	□	×
First Number	24		
Second Number	16		
Total	40		
		Add	

Try adding another **Button** to provide a clear facility with the statement Sum.Text="" in its Click event-handler.

Applying user values

While the Label control works great to display an assigned Text property value, it does not allow the user to directly input a value. The **TextBox** control does both and should be used instead of a Label control, where direct dynamic user input is desirable.

Replacing the Label controls named **Num1** and **Num2** in the previous example, with TextBox controls of the same name, allows the user to dynamically change those values used to compute the sum total value when the **Button** is clicked.

1 Click on **File**, **New**, **Project** to start a new **Windows Forms Application** and name it "UserInput"

2 From the ToolBox, add four **Label** controls, two **TextBox** controls, and two **Button** controls to the default Form

3 Use the **Properties** window to change the **Text** property value of the Form, Buttons, and Labels, and arrange their position so the interface looks something like this:

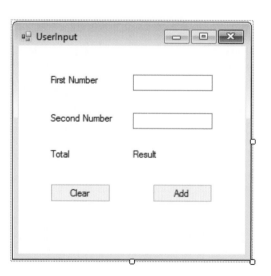

Hot tip

It is good programming practice to give meaningful names to all controls, for easy recognition – the name **AddBtn** makes a Button more easily recognizable than the name **Button1**.

4 To avoid confusion with other controls, use the Properties window to change the **(Name)** property of the two TextBox controls to **Num1** and **Num2**, the Button controls to **AddBtn** and **ClearBtn**, and the Label with the "Result" Text value to **Sum** – the new names can now be used in programming code to refer to these controls

5 Double-click the **AddBtn** to open the Code Editor within its Click event-handler and add the statement **Sum.Text = Val(Num1.Text) + Val(Num2.Text)**

6 Double-click the **ClearBtn** to open the Code Editor within its Click event-handler and add the statements **Sum.Text = "Result" : Num1.Text = "" : Num2.Text = ""**

Multiple statements can be added on a single line if they are separated from each other by a colon character.

7 Click on the **Start** button to run the application. Enter any numeric values you like into the TextBox fields, then click the **AddBtn** button to see the **Sum** total value

UserInput	—	□	×

First Number   22.5

Second Number   47.5

Total   70

Clear   Add

8 Click the **ClearBtn** button to assign new property values, resuming the application's initial state, and it is now ready to add two more input values

When typing code, there is no need to worry about capitals or lower case letters as Visual Basic is not case-sensitive.

33

Prompting for input

In addition to input via Form window controls, an application can seek user input from an **InputBox** dialog. This is similar to a **MsgBox** dialog but also has a text field where the user can type input that will be returned to the application. The user input value can then be assigned to a property in the usual way.

Unlike a simple code statement that calls up a MsgBox, just to advise the user, a statement that calls up an InputBox should make an assignation of the returned value.

Don't forget

Use the **Me** keyword to address the current Form – you can address controls on it by name.

1. Click on **File**, **New**, **Project** to start a new **Windows Forms Application** and name it "DialogInput"

2. From the ToolBox add a **Button** control to the Form

3. Double-click the Button to open the **Code Editor** within its **Click** event-handler and add the statement **Me.Text = InputBox("Enter a Caption...")**

4. Click the **Start** button to run the application, then click the Button to call up the InputBox

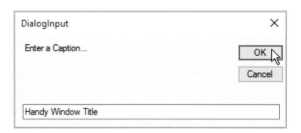

Hot tip

An **InputBox** statement should always contain an = assignment operator.

5. Enter any text you like into the input field, then click the **OK** button to assign the value of your input to the Form's **Text** property as a window title caption

34

InputBox title and default response

Notice that the **InputBox** title caption assumes the name of the application by default – in this case it's "DialogInput". You may, however, specify your own InputBox title by adding a second string after the message string within the parentheses.

Optionally, you may specify a default response that will appear in the text field when the InputBox is called by adding a third string within the parentheses. All strings must be separated by a comma.

1. In the DialogInput application, double-click the **Button** to reopen the **Code Editor** within its **Click** event-handler and edit the previous statement to read
**Me.Text = InputBox("Enter a Caption..." , _
"Caption Selector" , "Dandy Window Title")**

2. Click the **Start** button to run the application, then click the Button to call up the InputBox

3. Note the InputBox title caption, then click the **OK** button to assign the default response value to the Form's **Text** property as a window title caption

Specifying dialog properties

The features of a **MsgBox** dialog can be determined by adding a comma and specification value after the message string within its parentheses. This can specify which buttons the dialog will display and what graphic icon, if any, will appear on the dialog.

Button constant	Value
vbOkOnly	0
vbOkCancel	1
vbAbortRetryIgnore	2
vbYesNoCancel	3
vbYesNo	4
vbRetryCancel	5

The dialog button combinations can be specified using the Visual Basic constant values, or their numeric equivalents, as shown in this table. For example, to have the dialog display Yes, No, and Cancel buttons, specify the **vbYesNoCancel** constant or its numeric equivalent **3**.

Icon constant		Value
vbCritical	✖	16
vbQuestion	?	32
vbExclamation	!	48
vbInformation	i	64

The dialog icon can be specified using the Visual Basic constant values, or their numeric equivalents, as shown in this table. For example, to have the dialog display the question mark icon, specify the **vbQuestion** constant or its numeric equivalent **32**.

Always specify a graphic icon when calling a **MsgBox** dialog, to help the user easily understand the nature of the message.

In order to have the **MsgBox** display both a particular button combination and a certain graphic icon, the specification can add the button constant and the icon constant together using the addition + operator. For example, the specification to display Yes, No, and Cancel buttons along with a question icon would be **vbYesNoCancel + vbQuestion**. Alternatively, you can specify the sum total of their numeric equivalents – in this case it's **35** (3 + 32).

The buttons in a **MsgBox** dialog each return a specific numeric value to the application when they are clicked. This can be assigned to a property in much the same way as the value returned from the **InputBox** dialog in the previous example.

1 Click on **File**, **New**, **Project** to start a new **Windows Forms Application** and name it "MsgBoxDialog"

2 From the ToolBox add a **Button**, a **Label**, and a **TextBox** to the default Form and arrange them to your liking

3 Set the Label's **Text** property to "Button Value :" and name the TextBox **BtnValue**

4 Double-click the **Button** to open the **Code Editor** within its **Click** event-handler and add the statement **BtnValue. Text = MsgBox("Click any button" , _ vbYesNoCancel + vbQuestion)**

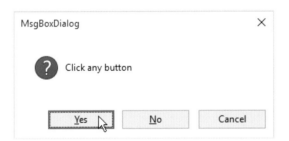

5 Press the **Start** button to run the application, then click any button and note the value it returns to the **TextBox**

Don't confuse the button return values with the Visual Basic constant values used to specify the button combinations.

Try changing the **MsgBox** combination specification using constant or numeric values – and make a note of the value returned by each button.

Summary

- In Visual Basic each object has a name and properties.
- When an object is selected in the Form Designer, the current value of each of its properties can be inspected in the **Properties** window.
- The value of any property can be edited in the **Properties** window to assign a new value to that property.
- Features determining the appearance of an application, such as **Font** and **Layout**, can be set at designtime along with content.
- Content, such as **Text** and **Color** values, can also be initialized at runtime using the Form's **Load** event-handler.
- **Control** objects placed on a Form can be addressed by their name, but you should use the **Me** keyword to address the current Form itself.
- Programming code can use existing property values in a calculation to compute a further value at runtime.
- **Label** controls merely display text, they do not allow user input.
- **TextBox** controls both display text and allow user input.
- It is recommended you give all controls a meaningful name for easy recognition.
- Visual Basic is not case-sensitive so no special care is needed to observe capital or lower case letters in code.
- An **InputBox** allows user input to be assigned to any property.
- Unlike a **MsgBox** statement, a call to the **InputBox** should always assign the value which will be returned.
- Optionally, a title and default response can be specified for an **InputBox** dialog.
- Optionally, a button combination and icon can be specified for a **MsgBox** dialog.

3 Using controls

This chapter illustrates how many of the Common Controls within the Visual Basic Toolbox can be used to develop an exciting application interface.

Tab order

When creating an application interface with multiple controls consider how it can be navigated without a mouse, by those users who prefer keyboard navigation. Typically, they will expect to be able to move the focus from one control to another by pressing the **Tab** key. It is, therefore, important to allow the focus to move in a logical order when the Tab key is pressed, by setting the **TabIndex** property values of your controls.

Hot tip

In Windows applications, the term "focus" describes which control is active. Pressing the **Enter** key is equivalent to clicking on the control in current focus.

1   Place several controls on a Form, then click on the one you want to be first in the **Tab** order to select it

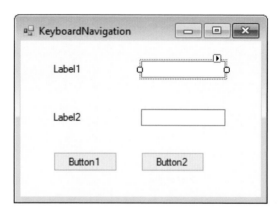

Don't forget

Not all controls can receive focus. The **Label** controls in this example are not able to get focus so the tab action just skips to the next control.

2   Set the **TabIndex** property value of the selected control to zero so it has first focus

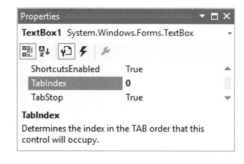

3   Repeat for other controls, setting each **TabIndex** with an ascending value – 1, 2, 3, and so on

4   Press the **Start** button to run the program, then hit the Tab key to see it follow your chosen order

Using Button

The **Button** control provides the user with an easy way to start an operation, confirm or cancel a choice, or get help. In Visual Basic, programming code needs to be added within each Button's event-handler to determine its function. Also, its properties need to be set to determine its appearance – Size, Text, Color, Font, etc. When setting the **Text** property, you can easily create an access key shortcut by prefixing the value with an ampersand **&** character.

 Select the Button control in the Form Designer then use the **Properties** window to modify its **Size** and **Color**

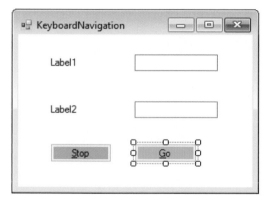

2 Assign a **Text** property value that is prefixed by an ampersand **&** character to create an access key shortcut

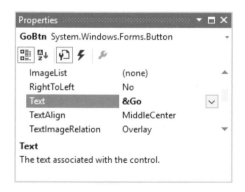

3 Add **MsgBox("Going")** code to the button's **Click** event-handler, then run the program and press **Alt + G** to test the "Go" button's access key

The **Enabled** property can be set to **False** to prevent a Button being available to the user until your program enables it.

The standard Windows look is familiar and comfortable for most users – avoid radical customization of your application.

Using TextBox

The **TextBox** control is an essential part of most applications, typically providing a single-line text input area for the user. Greater amounts of text input can be accommodated in a TextBox if its **MultiLine** property is set to **True**, and its **ScrollBars** property is set to **Vertical**.

Don't forget

Typing a space into a **TextBox** adds a space character.

1 Place a **TextBox** and a **Button** control onto a Form

2 Select the TextBox and use the **Properties** window to set its **ScrollBars** property to **Vertical**

3 Click on the **Smart Tag** arrowed button over the TextBox, or use the Properties window, to set its **MultiLine** property to **True**

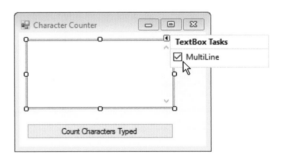

4 Add this statement to the Button's **Click** event-handler
```
MsgBox("You typed: " & _
Str ( Len ( TextBox1.Text ) ) & " characters" )
```

Hot tip

The ampersand **&** character is used in this example to concatenate (join) the code together.

5 Run the application, type some text into the **TextBox**, then click the **Button** to test the application

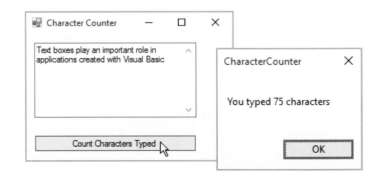

42

Using ComboBox

A **ComboBox** control can be used in place of a TextBox to provide an additional range of text values in a drop-down list. The user can choose one of the listed values to insert into the text field or type into it directly, just like a regular TextBox. The ComboBox provides a user-friendly list of anticipated input but occupies only the same space as a single-line TextBox.

1 Select the **ComboBox** control and find its **Items** property in the Properties window

2 Click the ellipsis (**...**) button in its value column to launch the **String Collection Editor**

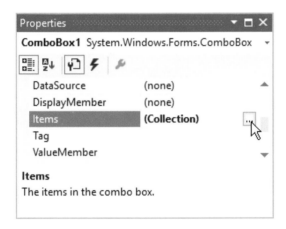

3 Enter a list of alternatives you wish to offer, adding one on each line, then click the **OK** button

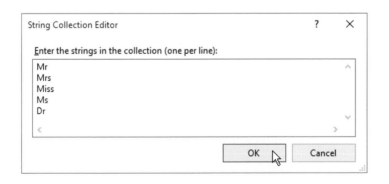

You can discover the value selected by the user from the ComboBox's **Text** property.

Using Label

A **Label** control is intended to advise the user, and provides a rectangular area that is generally used to provide text information. It can also provide simple rectangular graphics by displaying no text value, and setting its **AutoSize** and **BackColor** properties.

You can add an outline to a Label using its **BorderStyle** property.

1 Add three **Label** controls to a Form

2 Select each Label in turn and, in the **Properties** window, set the **AutoSize** property value to **False**

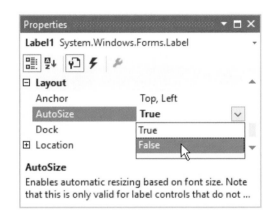

3 Select each Label in turn and, in the **Properties** window, set the **BackColor** property value to your preference

4 Select each Label in turn and, in the **Properties** window, delete the **Text** property value so it becomes blank

You can use the drop-down list in the **Properties** window to select a control to edit.

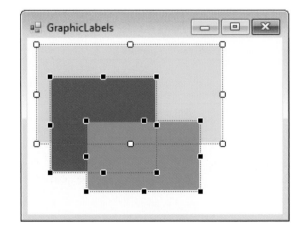

44

Using PictureBox

The **PictureBox** control allows images to be added to your application interface. These can be referenced as local files or imported into your application as a resource. Adding an image as a resource ensures your application will be portable when deployed, as it includes its own copy of the image.

1 Add a **PictureBox** control to a Form, and then select it

2 Find its **Image** property in the **Properties** window then click the ellipsis button [**...**] to launch the **Select Resource** dialog box

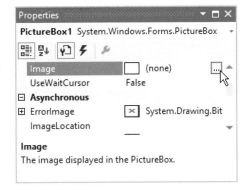

Beware

Acceptable image formats are Bitmap (**.bmp**), Icon (**.ico**), GIF (**.gif**), Metafile (**.wmf**), and JPEG (**.jpg**) – other formats cannot be imported unless they are converted first.

3 Check the **Project resource file:** radio button, then click **Import** to browse to the location of the image file

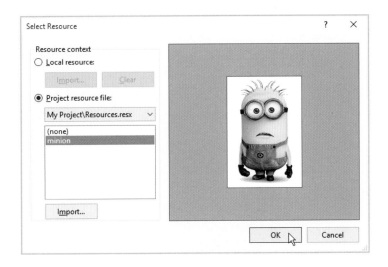

Hot tip

Notice after importing an image, the file gets added into the **Resources** folder in the **Solution Explorer** window.

4 Click **OK** to import the image file into your application and to place the image in the **PictureBox** control

Using ListBox

The Visual Basic **ListBox** is one of the most useful controls as it provides a convenient way to present multiple choices to the user. It allows large lists, of even several thousand items, to be displayed in a compact manner. Typically, the list data is derived from an external source, such as a database, then incorporated within your application – address books, business records, collections, etc.

Although the Properties window allows items to be added manually to a ListBox **Items** property, as with a ComboBox, it is often more appropriate to build the list dynamically by adding items at runtime – using the Form's **Load** event-handler.

You don't need to worry about setting **ListBox** scroll bars for longer lists – they get added automatically.

1 Add a **ListBox**, **Label**, and **Button** control to a Form

2 Name the ListBox "BookList" and change the **Text** property values of the Label and Button like this:

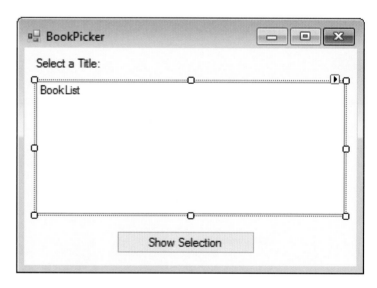

The items in this small list example are added in the code one by one. Larger lists, can be added more economically using a code loop – learn more about loops on page 68.

3 Double-click on the Form to open the Code Editor in the Form's **Load** event-handler and add the statement **BookList.Items.Add("HTML5 in easy steps")**

4 Repeat the above statement, each on a new line, substituting a different title within the parentheses for each title you want to add to the list

5 To have the list items sorted alphabetically, add the statement **BookList.Sorted = True**

6 To have the first item in the list selected by default, add the statement **BookList.SelectedIndex = 0**

7 To show the list length in the Form's caption, add the statement **Me.Text = BookList.Items.Count & _ " More Books by Mike McGrath"**

8 Return to the Form Designer and double-click the **Button** to open the **Code Editor** in its event-handler. To display the current selected list item when it is clicked, add the statement **MsgBox(BookList.Text)**

Beware

Remember that the first item in the index is numbered as zero, not 1.

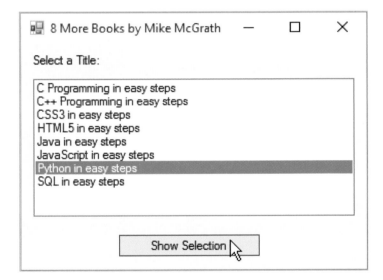

9 Run the application and see the first item appear selected. Select a different item, then click the **Button** to confirm the selection

Hot tip

The ListBox's **Sorted** property can also be set in the Properties window.

47

Using CheckBox

A **CheckBox** control is a small box with a caption. It lets the user select the caption choice by clicking on the box, and then a check mark appears in the box to indicate it has been chosen. Clicking the box once more deselects the choice and unchecks the box.

CheckBox controls are ideal to present a set of choices from which the user can select none, one, or more than one choice.

1 Add two **CheckBox** controls to a Form along with a **Label**, **ListBox**, and **Button**

2 Use the **Properties** window to change the **Text** property values of the CheckBox controls, Label, and Button to look like the ones below, and name the ListBox "Pizza"

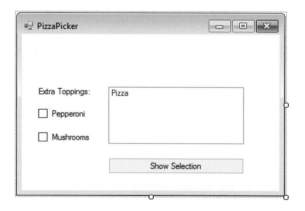

3 Add this statement to the Button's **Click** event-handler to clear the list box when it's clicked **Pizza.Items.Clear()**

4 Now, add these statements to add list items for each checked CheckBox control

```
If CheckBox1.Checked = True Then
        Pizza.Items.Add( Checkbox1.Text )
End If

If CheckBox2.Checked = True Then
        Pizza.Items.Add( Checkbox2.Text )
End If
```

48

Using RadioButton

A **RadioButton** control is like a CheckBox, but with one crucial difference – the user can check only one choice in the group. Checking a RadioButton automatically unchecks any others.

RadioButton controls are ideal to present a set of choices from which the user can select only one choice.

1 Add two **RadioButton** controls and a **Label** to the Form opposite, then edit their **Text** properties to look like this:

2 Insert these statements in the Button's **Click** event-handler, straight after the clear instruction

```
If RadioButton1.Checked = True Then
        Pizza.Items.Add( RadioButton1.Text )
End If

If RadioButton2.Checked = True Then
        Pizza.Items.Add( RadioButton2.Text )
End If
```

3 Run the application, select various choices, then click the **Button** to test the selection results

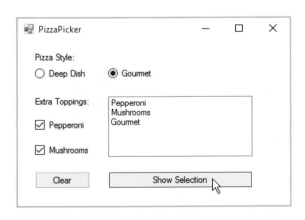

When creating **RadioButton** groups, always set one choice as the default by changing its **Checked** property value to **True** in the Properties window.

Hot tip

Try adding a Clear button to the Form. This will clear the **ListBox** and all selected choices when it gets clicked.

Using WebBrowser

The Visual Basic **WebBrowser** control makes it a snap to quickly add a document viewer to your application that can view HTML documents both online, and on your own computer. It can also display plain text and image files – just like your web browser.

1 Add a **WebBrowser** control to a Form – it will automatically occupy the entire Form area

2 Click on the **Smart Tag** arrow button and select the link to **Undock in Parent Container**

3 Add a **TextBox** and **Button** control, then arrange the Form controls to look like this:

Grab the handles around the controls to resize them on the Form.

4 Double-click the **Button** to open the **Code Editor** in its event-handler, then add the following statement
WebBrowser1.Navigate(TextBox1.Text)

5 Run the application, type a valid URL into the **TextBox** field, then click the **Button** to view the web page

The **Enter** key will not activate the button's **Click** event unless you add an access key shortcut.

6 Type a valid local file address into the **TextBox** field and click the **Button** to view it in the **WebBrowser** control

Using Timer

The **Timer** is an invisible control that can be found in the **Components** section of the Visual Studio **ToolBox**. When added to your application, it fires an event at a regular interval set by you. Statements within the Timer's event-handler are then executed whenever the **Timer** event occurs.

Hot tip

Set the **PictureBox** controls to **AutoSize** using the Smart Tags or the Properties window.

1 Add two **PictureBox** controls and a **Button** to a Form

2 Assign two similar images of the same size to the **PictureBox** controls, then hold down the **Shift** key while you click on each to select both together

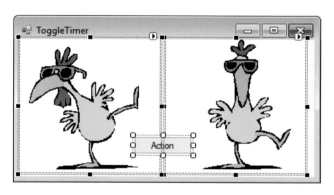

Beware

Controls can be accidentally repositioned – use **Lock Controls** under the **Format** menu to be sure they stay put.

3 On the menu bar, select **Format**, **Align**, **Centers** to exactly align the PictureBox controls one above the other

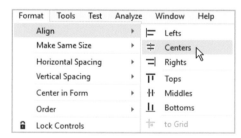

4 Select **Format, Order, Bring to Front** or **Send to Back** to ensure that PictureBox1 is at the front (on top) of the PictureBox2 control – click on the top one and check the current selected control name in the **Properties** window

5 Add a **Timer** control to the Form from the **Components** section of the ToolBox – its icon appears on the **Component Tray** at the bottom of the Form Designer

6 Double-click on the Timer icon to open the **Code Editor** at its **Tick** event-handler, then add these statements
```
If PictureBox1.Visible = True Then
        PictureBox1.Visible = False
Else
        PictureBox1.Visible = True
End If
```

This code inspects the **Visible** property of the top **PictureBox** and "toggles" its visibility on and off – like flicking a light switch

7 Double-click the **Button** to open the **Code Editor** at its event-handler, then add these statements
```
If Timer1.Enabled = False Then
        Timer1.Enabled = True
Else
        Timer1.Enabled = False
End If
```

This code inspects the **Enabled** property of the **Timer** and "toggles" it on and off when the **Button** gets clicked

8 Run the application then click the **Button** to watch the Timer appear to animate the PictureBox images

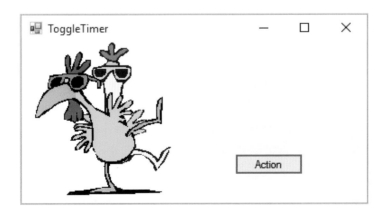

The popular controls demonstrated in this chapter are just some of the many controls available in the **ToolBox** – experiment with each one to understand them.

You can adjust the Timer's **Interval** property value to change the speed of the animation.

Summary

- The **TabIndex** property determines the order in which a user can navigate around the interface controls with the **Tab** key.

- Access key shortcuts are assigned to Buttons by prefixing the **Text** property value with an ampersand **&** character.

- **TextBox** controls can usefully display multiple lines of text if their **MultiLine** property is set to **True** and their **ScrollBars** property is set to **Vertical**.

- A **ComboBox** control allows typed text input, like a TextBox, plus it offers the user a list of anticipated input items to click.

- **Label** controls contain text information and do not allow focus or direct input. They can, however, be useful to provide simple rectangular graphics.

- A **PictureBox** control allows an image to be incorporated in the application interface.

- Importing images as a resource ensures that the application will be portable when it is deployed.

- **ListBox** controls are useful to compactly display numerous data items – both from within the program, and from external sources such as a database.

- **CheckBox** controls let the user choose none, one, or more options, whereas **RadioButton** controls let the user choose just one option from a group.

- A **WebBrowser** control can display HTML documents plus plain text and images – just like your regular web browser.

- You can use a **Timer** control to create an event in your application that fires at a regular interval set by you.

- The toggle technique is useful in Visual Basic programming to alternate a **Property** value.

4 Learning the language

This chapter demonstrates the mechanics of the Visual Basic programming language which allow data to be stored, controlled, and manipulated, to progress the application.

The examples in this chapter demonstrate the various elements of a program. Refer back to these for identification.

The Visual Basic IDE is a safe environment in which to experiment and learn from your mistakes.

Elements of a program

A program is simply a series of instructions that tell the computer what to do. Although programs can be complex, each individual instruction is generally simple. The computer starts at the beginning and works through, line by line, until it gets to the end. Here are some of the essential elements in Visual Basic:

Statements

A statement is an instruction that performs an action. For example, the statement **Lbl.BackColor = Color.Blue** sets the background color of **Lbl** to **Blue**.

Functions

A function is a statement that returns a value. For example, the function **InputBox()** returns the value of its dialog text field.

Variables

A variable is a word defined in the program that stores a value. For example, the statement **msg = "Hello World!"** stores a string of characters in a variable called **msg**.

Operators

An operator is an arithmetical symbol. For example, the * asterisk character is the multiplication operator and the / forward slash character is the division operator.

Objects

An object is a program "building block" entity. It can be visible, like a Button control, or invisible like a Timer control.

Properties

A property is a characteristic of an object. For example, the property **Btn.Text** is the **Text** property of the **Btn** object.

Methods

A method is an action that an object can perform. For example, the method **Btn.Click()** is the **Click** method of the **Btn** object.

Comments

A comment is an explanatory line in the program code starting with an apostrophe ' character. It's not actually read by the compiler but exists to explain the purpose of the code. For example, ' **Clear the list**. might explain a **Clear** statement.

…cont'd

The illustration below shows the **Code Editor** view of Visual
Basic programming code, for the **Click** event-handler of a **Button**
control – line numbering is turned on to aid analysis of the code.

Hot tip

To turn on line
numbering, click on
Tools, **Options**, then
expand **Text Editor**,
Basic. Choose **General**
then check the **Line
Numbers** option.

Line-by-line analysis

- Lines 1 and 16 – start and end of the entire Form code
- Lines 3 and 14 – start and end of the Button event-handler
- Lines 5, 8, and 11 – explanatory comments
- Line 6 – creates a variable called **msg** to store String data
- Line 9 – places text value into the **msg** variable
- Line 12 – calls the **MsgBox()** function to show the **msg** value

Syntax highlighting

Beware

- **Keywords** – Visual Basic core language words appear in blue
- **Strings** – text values, within double-quotes, appear in red
- **Comments** – explanatory lines appear in green
- **Code** – everything else appears in **black**

The syntax colors
shown here are the
default colors. Custom
colors can be chosen
in the **Tools**, **Options**
dialog, by expanding
Environment, **Fonts
and Colors**.

Declaring variable types

A variable is like a container in a program where a data value can be stored. It is called a variable because its contents can change (vary) during the course of the program.

You can create a variable by typing a declaration comprising the Visual Basic **Dim** keyword followed by a unique variable name of your choice. For example, **Dim msg** declares a new variable with the name **msg**.

The variable declaration should also specify the type of data the variable can store using the **As** keyword followed by one of the Visual Basic data types. So, **Dim msg As String** declares a new variable called **msg** that can store a string of characters.

There are many data types available in Visual Basic programming but those most frequently used are listed in the table below:

Hot tip

Always choose a meaningful name for your variable to aid its easy recognition.

Data type	Possible value
Boolean	True or False
String	Characters
Integer	Whole number
Double	Floating-point number

After a variable has been created with a specified data type, it can only store data of the type specified in the declaration. For example, you cannot assign a **String** to an **Integer** variable.

Data, of the appropriate type, can be assigned to the variable at any point in the program. A variable declaration can also initialize a variable. For example, **Dim msg As String = "Hello"** initializes a new **String** variable called **msg** with the value **Hello**.

Don't forget

Any value within double quotes is a **String** – so "123" is a **String**, and the content of a **TextBox** is also a **String**.

...cont'd

Specifying data types for variables has several advantages:

- It lets you perform specialized tasks for each data type – character manipulation with **String** values, validation with **Boolean** values, and arithmetic with **Integer** and **Double** values.
- It enables **IntelliSense** to pop up their features as you type.
- It takes advantage of compiler type checking to prevent errors.
- It results in faster execution of your code.

You can easily display the value stored in any variable, by assigning it to the text-based property of visual control, such as a ListBox.

1 Add a **ListBox** control and a **Button** control to a Form

2 Double-click the Button to launch the **Code Editor** in its event-handler

3 Add these lines to declare and initialize four variables
```
Dim bool As Boolean = False
Dim str As String = "Some text"
Dim int As Integer = 1000
Dim num As Double = 7.5
```

4 Now, add these lines to display the stored values
```
ListBox1.Items.Add( "bool value is " & bool )
ListBox1.Items.Add( "str value is " & str )
ListBox1.Items.Add( "int value is " & int )
ListBox1.Items.Add( "num value is " & num )
```

5 Run the application and click the **Button** to see the value stored in each variable

IntelliSense is the pop-up box that appears as you type in the **Code Editor**, showing code features.

Two useful functions are **Str()**, that converts a number to a string, and **Val()**, that converts a string to a number. The **Str()** function was seen in action on page 42 and **Val()** back on page 31.

Understanding variable scope

The accessibility of a variable is known as its "scope", and depends upon where its declaration is made in the program. A variable's scope determines which parts of the program are able to inspect or change the value stored in that variable.

Variables that are declared within a **Sub** routine section of code, such as an event-handler, are only accessible within that routine. Reference to them from outside that routine will result in an error as they will not be visible from other routines. A variable declared within a **Sub** routine is, therefore, said to have "local" scope – it is only accessible locally within that routine.

Local variables are generally declared with the **Dim** keyword, a given name, and a data type specification. The given name must be unique within its own scope but can be used again for another local variable of different scope. For example, two different event-handler **Sub** routines may both declare a local variable called **msg**. There is no conflict here as each one is invisible to the other.

Hot tip

Notice that the first line of an event-handler begins with the keywords **Private Sub** – identifying it as a **Sub** routine.

1. Add three **Button** controls to a Form

2. Double-click on the first **Button** to open the **Code Editor** in its event-handler and add this code
   ```
   Dim msg As String = "Hello from the Button1 Sub"
   MsgBox( msg )
   ```

3. Double-click on the second **Button** and add this code to its event-handler, which also declares a **msg** variable
   ```
   Dim msg As String = "Hello from the Button2 Sub"
   MsgBox( msg )
   ```

4. Run the application and click each **Button** to confirm the value in each **msg** variable is retrieved without conflict

Beware

Visual Basic projects have a compiler setting called **Option Explicit** that can enforce proper variable declaration, as described here. Always leave this set to **On** (its default setting), so you will be obliged to declare variables correctly.

VarScope ✕

Hello from the Button1 Sub

OK

VarScope ✕

Hello from the Button2 Sub

OK

...cont'd

You may often want a variable to be accessible by more than one **Sub** routine in your program, so its declaration will need to be made outside of any **Sub** routine code. It should, instead, appear in the Form declarations section, right after the Form **Class** line at the start of the code. Variables may be declared here with either the **Private** or **Dim** keyword to become accessible throughout the entire Form scope – so any **Sub** routine can reference them.

The Form Declaration section may also contain variable declarations made with the **Public** keyword, to be accessible throughout the entire project, including other Form modules. These are known as "global" variables because they are accessible from absolutely anywhere.

Variable names must be unique within their visible scope.

5 In the **Code Editor**, type these declarations into the Form declarations section, at the top of the code
Public globalVar As String = "Hello from the Project"
Private formVar As String = "Hello from this Module"

6 Add this line to the third **Button** control's event-handler
MsgBox(globalVar & vbCrLf & formVar)

7 Run the application and click on the third **Button** to retrieve the values from the project-wide and module-wide variables

In deciding where best to declare a variable, always make it as local as possible to avoid errors – your first choice should be a local **Dim** declaration, then a **Private** module declaration, then a **Public** global declaration.

Working with variable arrays

The variables introduced so far let you store just one value, but sometimes it's more convenient to deal with a set of values. For example, you might want to store the monthly sales figures for a quarterly period. Rather than create three separate variables named **JanSales**, **FebSales**, and **MarSales**, you can create a single variable array named **Sales** with three elements – one for each month. You can refer to them as **Sales(0)**, **Sales(1)**, and **Sales(2)**.

Don't forget

Array indexing begins at zero by default – so the last element of an array of three elements is numbered 2, not 3.

1 Add a **Button** to a Form then create an array variable of three elements in its **Click** event-handler with this code
Dim Sales(2) As Double

2 Assign values to each element in turn
Sales(0) = 5245.00
Sales(1) = 4785.00
Sales(2) = 7365.50

3 Create a regular variable then assign it the total value of all three array elements
Dim Quarter As Double
Quarter = Sales(0) + Sales(1) +Sales(2)

4 Finally, add a statement to display the total value, formatted by the computer's regional currency settings
MsgBox("Quarter Sales:" & FormatCurrency(Quarter))

Beware

Do not attempt to reference a non-existent array element number in your code. In this example **Sales(3)** creates an **Out Of Range** error.

5 Run the application to test the result. It is shown here producing the total value formatted in dollars, but the formatting depends on the regional settings of the computer on which the application is running

> VarArray   ×
>
> Quarter Sales:$17,395.50
>
> OK

You may, if you wish, initialize the array elements in its declaration without explicitly specifying the number of elements. The values should be assigned as a comma-separated list within curly braces. In this example the declaration would be
Dim Sales() As Double = { 5245.0, 4785.0, 7365.5 }

Multi-dimensional arrays

Arrays can have more than one dimension. For example, you could create a 2-dimensional array to store the monthly sales of two stores over a quarterly period with **Dim Sales(2,1) As Double**. Individual elements can then be referenced as **Sales(0,0)**, **Sales(1,0)**, **Sales(2,0)**, **Sales(0,1)**, **Sales(1,1)**, and **Sales(2,1)**.

1 Add a **Button** to a Form, then create an array variable of 3x2 elements in its **Click** event-handler with this code
Dim Sales(2,1) As Double

2 Assign values to each element in turn
Sales(0,0) = 1255 : Sales(1,0) = 1845.5 : Sales(2,0) =1065
Sales(0,1) = 2175 : Sales(1,1) = 2215.5 : Sales(2,1) = 2453

3 Create two regular variables. Assign one the total value of all elements in the array's first dimension, and the other the total value of all elements in its second dimension
Dim Store1, Store2 As Double
Store1 = Sales(0,0) + Sales(1,0) +Sales(2,0)
Store2 = Sales(0,1) + Sales(1,1) +Sales(2,1)

4 Finally, add a statement to display the total values, formatted by the computer's regional currency settings
MsgBox("Quarter Sales..." & vbCrLf & _
"Store 1 : " & FormatCurrency(Store1) & vbCrLf & _
"Store 2 : " & FormatCurrency(Store2))

5 Run the application to test the result. It is shown here producing the total values formatted in dollars but the formatting depends on the regional settings of the host computer

VarArray ✕

Quarter Sales...
Store1 : $4,165.50
Store2 : $6,843.50

OK

Beware

Arrays of two dimensions represent a square and those of three dimensions represent a cube, but arrays of more than three dimensions are best avoided as they are difficult to visualize.

Hot tip

Notice how the _ underscore character and **vbCrLf** constant are used here to format the **MsgBox** message.

Performing operations

The Visual Basic arithmetic operators listed in the table below are used to return the result of a calculation.

Operator	Description	Example
+	Addition	**16 + 4**
-	Subtraction	**16 - 4**
*	Multiplication	**16 * 4**
/	Division	**16 / 4**

In statements using more than one arithmetic operator, it is important to specify operator precedence to clarify the expression. For example, the expression **6 * 3 + 5** could return **48 (6 * 8)** or **23 (18 + 5)** – depending which arithmetic is performed first. Adding parentheses around the part you wish to perform first, clarifies the expression, so that **(6 * 3) + 5** assures the result will be **23 (18 + 5)**.

The Visual Basic comparison operators listed in the table below are used to test an expression and return a **True** or **False** result.

Beware

In Visual Basic the **=** symbol is used both to assign values, and to test for equality – other programming languages have a separate **==** equality operator.

Operator	Description	Example
=	Equality	**num = 10**
<>	Inequality	**num <> 10**
>	Greater than	**num > 10**
>=	Greater than or equal to	**num >= 10**
<	Less than	**num < 10**
<=	Less than or equal to	**num <= 10**

...cont'd

The Visual Basic arithmetic operators can be used to easily create simple calculation functionality in your application.

1 Add two **TextBox**, four **Button**, and three **Label** controls to a Form, and arrange them as below

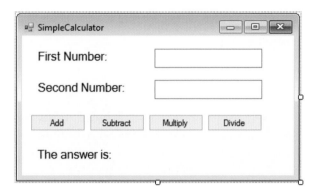

2 Double-click the "Add" button to open the **Code Editor** in its event-handler, then type this statement
Label3.Text = "The answer is : " & _
Str(Val(TextBox1.Text) + Val(TextBox2.Text))

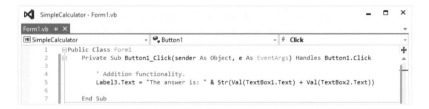

3 Repeat step 2 for the other **Button** controls but replace the + operator with the appropriate arithmetic operator: - for subtraction, / for division, and * for multiplication

4 Run the application and enter two numbers, say 16 and 4, into the **TextBox** fields, then click each **Button** control

Other Visual Basic operators include the ampersand **&** which is used to concatenate (join) code, and the underscore _ which lets statements continue on the next line.

Branching code

Making statements that test an expression allows the program to perform one action or another, according to the result of the test. This important technique is known as "conditional branching" – the code will branch one way or another, depending on whether a condition is **True** or **False**. In Visual Basic, conditional branching can be performed by an **If** statement, using this syntax:

```
If ( test-expression-returns-True ) Then
        execute-this-statement
Else
        execute-this-alternative-statement
End If
```

Optionally, multiple expressions can be included in the test using the **And** keyword, where both expressions must be **True**, or the **Or** keyword where either one of the expressions must be **True**.

An **If** statement must always end with the **End If** keywords.

1   Add a **Label** control to a Form

2   Double-click on the Form to open the **Code Editor** in the Form's **Load** event-handler

3   Type the following If statement to assign an appropriate value to the Label control, according to whether either of the two tested expressions is True

```
If ( WeekDay( Now ) = vbSaturday ) Or _
( WeekDay( Now ) = vbSunday ) Then
        Label1.Text = "Relax – it's the weekend"
Else
        Label1.Text = "Today's a working weekday"
End If
```

If statements were used back on page 53 to toggle property values, and on page 48, without the optional **Else** part, to test the status of **CheckBox** and **RadioButton** controls.

4   Run the application – the message will vary depending on whether the current day is a weekday or a weekend day

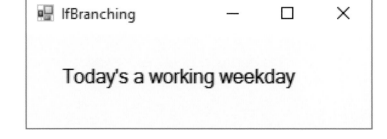

Conditional branching can also be performed with a **Select Case** statement, to provide multiple possible branches, using this syntax:

```
Select Case expression-to-test
Case Is test-returns-True
        execute-this-statement-then-exit
Case Is test-returns-True
        execute-this-statement-then-exit
Case Else
        execute-this-default-statement
End Select
```

You can add as many **Case** tests as you wish and, optionally, use **Case Else** to provide a final default statement, to be executed when none of the tests return **True**.

1 Add a **Label** control to a Form

2 Double-click on the Form to open the **Code Editor** in the Form's **Load** event-handler

3 Type the following statement to assign an appropriate value to the Label control according to which of the tested expressions is true

```
Select Case WeekDay( Now )
Case Is = vbSaturday
        Label1.text = "It's a Super Saturday"
Case Is = vbSunday
        Label1.Text = "It's a Lazy Sunday"
Case Else
        Label1.text = "It's just another working day"
End Select
```

4 Run the application to see an appropriate message

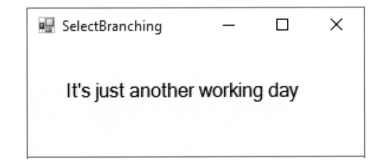

Try using a **Select Case** statement to branch code according to the value returned from a **MsgBox** dialog, with Yes, No, and Cancel buttons – as seen on page 36/37.

An **If** statement must always end with **End If** keywords and a **Select Case** statement with the **End Select** keywords.

67

Looping code

Programming loops allow statements within the loop to be executed repeatedly until the loop ends. They must always include a test expression to determine when to end – or they will run forever! The most popular loop in Visual Basic is the **For Next** loop, which uses a counter to test the number of times it has executed (iterated) its statements, and has this syntax:

For *counter* = *start* **To** *end*
       execute-this-statement
Next *update-the-counter*

It is often useful to incorporate the increasing value of the counter into the statement/s executed on each iteration of the loop.

1   Add a **TextBox**, **Button**, and **ListBox** control to a Form

2   Double-click the Button to open the **Code Editor** in its **Click** event-handler, then type this loop

```
Dim amount As Double = Val( TextBox1.Text )
Dim counter As Integer
For counter = 1 To 10
        ListBox1.Items.Add( "At " & counter & _
        "% interest is " & _
        FormatCurrency( (amount * counter) / 100 ) )
Next counter
```

3   Run the application, enter a number in the **TextBox**, then click the **Button** to run the loop

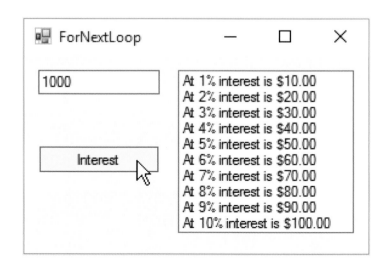

Beware

The counter variable stores the loop index – do not assign it any other value in the loop.

Other types of loop possible in Visual Basic are the **Do Until** loop and the **Do While** loop. Although similar, these two loops are subtly different – a **Do Until** loop executes its statements until the test expression becomes **True**, whereas the **Do While** loop executes its statements until the test expression becomes **False**.

All loops work well to iterate lists of data, and are especially useful to iterate the values contained in array elements.

1 Add a **ListBox** control to a Form

2 Double-click on the Form to open the **Code Editor** in its **Load** event-handler, then create this array
```
Dim Sales() As Double = { 5601, 8502, 6703, 4204, _
7605, 8206, 9107, 6508, 7209, 5010, 8011, 7012 }
```

3 Create a **String** variable with **Dim sum As String**

4 Now, type this loop, then run the application
```
Dim counter As Integer
Do Until counter = Sales.Length
        sum = FormatCurrency( Sales( counter ) )
        counter = counter + 1
        sum = sum & vbTab & MonthName( counter )
        ListBox1.Items.Add( sum )
Loop
```

DoUntilLoop	
$5,601.00	January
$8,502.00	February
$6,703.00	March
$4,204.00	April
$7,605.00	May
$8,206.00	June
$9,107.00	July
$6,508.00	August
$7,209.00	September
$5,010.00	October
$8,011.00	November
$7,012.00	December

Choose the **Do** loop which offers greater clarity for your particular purpose – but remember, they must both contain a statement to change the counter, and end with the Loop keyword.

The limit of this loop is specified by the **Length** property of the array. The counter references each element (0-11) from the **Sales** array and also each month name (1-12) from the Visual Basic **MonthName** function.

Calling object methods

Visual Basic objects have methods that can be called in code to make the object perform an action at runtime. This works in much the same way as when you can write code to assign property values to dynamically change an object's characteristics.

To view any object's available properties and methods' type its name followed by a period into the **Code Editor**. An "IntelliSense" pop-up window will appear showing all of that object's properties and methods. Scroll down the list, then double-click on an item to add that property or method into the code.

1 Add two **Label** and five **Button** controls to a Form

2 In the **Properties** window, set each Label's **AutoSize** to **False**, and delete their default **Text** value

3 Make the **BackColor** of one Label red and name it **RedLbl**, then set the other Label's **BackColor** to yellow

4 Edit the **Text** property of each **Button**, then arrange the controls so the Form looks like this:

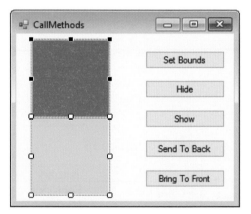

Leaving the **AutoSize** property set to the default of **True** prevents the **Label** being resized.

5 Double-click on the "Set Bounds" Button to open the **Code Editor** in its event-handler, then type **RedLbl.**

70

6. Find the **SetBounds** method in the **IntelliSense** window, then double-click it to add it to the code

7. The **SetBounds** method sets the size and position of the control using X, Y, Width, and Height. Add the settings **(45, 45, 45, 100)** to the code, right after the method name

8. Repeat for the other **Button** controls, adding calls to the **Hide()**, **Show()**, **BringToFront()**, and **SendToBack()** methods – no settings are required for any of these

9. Run the application and click each **Button** to try its action – see the stacking order change from back to front

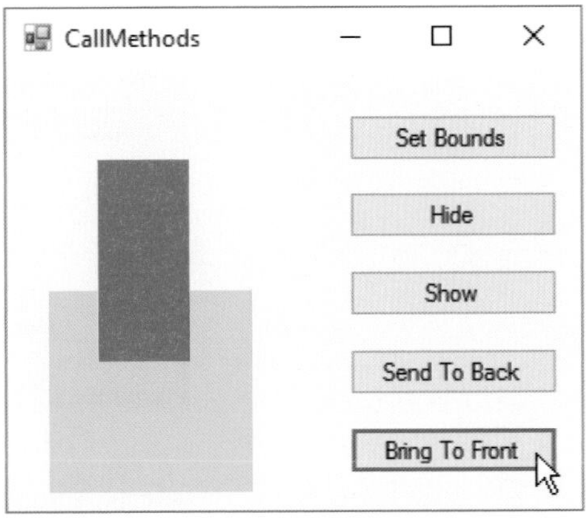

Don't forget

When you select an item in the **IntelliSense** window, a Tooltip appears containing that item's definition.

Using the With block shorthand

When creating code addressing several properties or methods of an object, it can be tedious to repeatedly type the object name.

```
BlueLbl.AutoSize = False
BlueLbl.BackColor = Color.Blue
BlueLbl.Width = 50
Blue.Lbl.Height = 50
BlueLbl.SendtoBack()
```

Usefully, a **With** block can neatly specify all the values and calls:

```
With BlueLbl
        .AutoSize = False
        .BackColor = Color.Blue
        .Width = 50
        .Height = 50
        .SendToBack()
End With
```

Hot tip

Try adding another **Label** to this example then set its properties and methods in the Form's **Load** event using a **With** block.

Creating a sub method

When you double-click on a **Form** or **Button** to open the **Code Editor**, you see that each event-handler begins and ends like this:

Private Sub ... End Sub

"Sub" is short for "subroutine" and each event-handler subroutine is a **Private** method of that Form's **Class**. You can create your own subroutine method from scratch, which can be called from other code in your application, as required.

Beware

All executable code must be contained inside a procedure, such as a **Sub** routine or a **Function**.

1 Add **Label**, **Button**, and **TextBox** controls to a Form, then arrange them like this:

72

Hot tip

If you find yourself writing similar code at several points in your application, consider creating a **Sub** routine to make your code more efficient, and easier to maintain.

2 Click on **View, Code** to open the **Code Editor**, then type this code into the declarations section
```
Private Sub ClearForm()
        TextBox1.Text = ""
        TextBox2.Text = ""
        TextBox3.Text = ""
End Sub
```

3 Click on **View, Designer** to return to the **Form Designer**, then double-click on the "Clear" **Button** to open the **Code Editor** in its **Click** event-handler

4 Type **Me.** and notice that the new **ClearForm** method has been added to the **IntelliSense** window. Double-click on it to add **Me.ClearForm()** to the code

5 Run the application, type some text into all three text fields, then click the "Clear" **Button** to clear the fields

Sending parameters

A powerful feature of **Sub** routines is their ability to receive information as they are called. This information is known as "parameters" and is sent from the parentheses of the calling statement to the parentheses of the **Sub** routine.

In order for a **Sub** routine to handle parameters, it must specify a name and data type for each parameter it is to receive. For example, **seq As String** would receive a single string parameter from the caller – it cannot be called unless one string is passed. The **Sub** routine code can then refer to the passed value using the given name, in this case **seq**. Multiple parameters can be passed if the **Sub** routine specifies the correct number and data types.

You can make a **Sub** routine accessible globally by changing its access modifier from **Private** to **Public**.

① Click **Stop Debugging** to return to the Form window shown opposite

② Now, click on **View, Code** to open the **Code Editor**, then type this code into the declarations section
```
Private Sub Customer(name As String, addr As String)
        TextBox1.Text = name
        TextBox2.Text = addr
End Sub
```

③ Edit the "Customer" **Button** control's **Click** event-handler to include this call to the new **Sub** routine
```
Me.Customer( "Mike McGrath", "1 Main Street, USA" )
```

④ Run the application and click the "Customer" **Button**

Try adding a third parameter to set the "Phone" number field.

Creating a function

A **Function** is similar to a **Sub** routine, but with one important difference – a **Function** returns a value to the caller. This means that you must specify the data type of the return value, in addition to specifying parameters, when creating a **Function**.

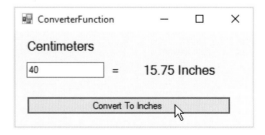
1. Add a **Button**, a **TextBox**, and three **Label** controls to a Form, and then arrange them like this:

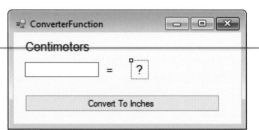

2. Click on **View, Code** to open the **Code Editor**, then type this code into the declarations section

```
Private Function Inches(ByVal Cm As String) As Double
    Inches = Cm / 2.54
    Inches = FormatNumber( Inches , 2 )
    Return Inches
End Function
```

The parentheses specify that the parameter **Inches** must be a **String** data type – this value is used in the calculation. The result is assigned to the **Function** name for return as a **Double** data type, formatted to just two decimal places.

3. Add a call to the "Inches" **Function** in the Button's **Click** event-handler **Sub** routine

```
Label1.Text = Inches(TextBox1.Text) & " Inches"
```

4. Run the application, enter a number, then click the **Button** to use the **Function**

Doing mathematics

The Visual Basic **Math** object has many methods that are useful when performing mathematical calculations. The most frequently used methods are listed below, together with examples returns.

Data type	Description
Math.Ceiling()	Rounds a number up, e.g. Math.Ceiling(3.5) returns 4
Math.Floor()	Rounds a number down, e.g. Math.Floor(3.5) returns 3
Math.Round()	Rounds to the nearest integer, e.g. Math.Round(3.5) returns 4
Math.Sqrt()	Returns the square root, e.g. Math.Sqrt(16) returns 4
Math.Max()	Returns the larger of two numbers, e.g. Math.Max(8, 64) returns 64
Math.Min()	Returns the smaller of two numbers, e.g. Math.Min(8, 64) returns 8
Math.Pow()	Returns a number raised to the specified power, e.g. Math.Pow(5, 2) returns 25
Math.Abs()	Returns an absolute value, e.g. Math.Abs(10.0) returns 10
Math.Cos()	Returns a cosine value, e.g. Math.Cos(10.0) returns -0.839
Math.Log()	Returns a natural logarithm, e.g. Math.Log(10.0) returns 2.303
Math.Sin()	Returns a sine value, e.g. Math.Sin(10.0) returns -0.544
Math.Tan()	Returns a tangent value, e.g. Math.Tan(10.0) returns 0.648

The **Math** class also has a **Math.PI** constant, representing the value of π – approximately 3.142.

The returns shown here for **Cosine**, **Log**, **Sine**, and **Tangent** are rounded to three decimal places – the actual returns provide greater precision.

Generating a random number

Random numbers can be generated by the Visual Basic **Rnd()** function, that returns a floating-point value between 0.0 and 1.0. Multiplying the random numbers will specify a wider range. For example, a multiplier of 20 will create a random number between zero and 20. To make the generated random number more useful, you can round it up to the nearest higher integer value with the **Math.Ceiling()** method so the range, in this case, becomes from 1 to 20.

The numbers generated by **Rnd()** are not truly random, but are merely a sequence of pseudo random numbers produced by an algorithm from a specific starting point. Whenever an application loads, a call to the **Rnd()** function will begin at the same starting point – so the same sequence will be repeated. This is not generally desirable, so the application needs to create a new starting point when it loads to avoid repetition. This can be achieved by calling the **Randomize()** function in the Form's **Load** event, to "seed" the **Rnd()** function with a starting point based upon the system time when the application gets loaded – now the sequence of generated numbers is different each time.

Beware

The numbers generated by the algorithm for **Randomize()** and **Rnd()** may be predicted, so this technique should not be used for cryptography.

Don't forget

Text in a **Label** will not wrap to the next line unless **AutoSize** is **False**.

1 Add a **Label**, **TextBox**, and **Button** control to a Form, and arrange them like this:

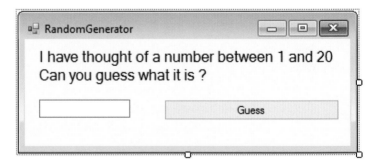

2 Name the **Label** control **Msg**, set its **AutoSize** property to **False**, then assign the text illustrated above to its **Text** property

3 Name the **TextBox** control **Guess**, and set the **Text** property of the **Button** likewise

4 Click on **View, Code** to open the **Code Editor**, then create a variable in the Declarations
```
Dim num As Integer
```

5 Still in the declarations section, add a **Sub** routine to assign a random number 1-20 to the **num** variable
```
Private Sub GetNumber()
        num = Math.Ceiling( Rnd() * 20 )
End Sub
```

The integer value must be extracted from the **TextBox** by the **Val()** function before making any comparison.

6 In the Form's **Load** event-handler, add a call to seed the random number generator and a call to set the **num** variable with an initial pseudo random value
```
Randomize()
GetNumber()
```

7 Now, add some logic to the **Button** control's **Click** event-handler with this code
```
Select Case ( Val( Guess.Text) )
Case Is > num
        Msg.text = Guess.Text & " is too high"
Case Is < num
        Msg.Text = Guess.Text & " is too low"
Case Is = num
        Msg.Text = Guess.Text & " is correct" & _
        "I have thought of another number - Try again!"
        GetNumber()
End Select
Guess.Text = ""
```

You can use the **vbCrLf** constant to format the contents of the **Label**.

8 Run the application and guess the random number

Summary

- A program's essential elements are: Statements, Variables, Functions, Operators, object Properties, and object Methods.
- Comment lines help to explain the purpose of the code.
- Variable declarations create a variable, and can begin with the **Dim**, **Public**, or **Private** keywords.
- Each variable declaration should specify the type of data that variable may contain along with the **As** keyword and a data type.
- **String**, **Integer**, **Double**, and **Boolean** are common data types.
- Numbers can be extracted from a **String** by the **Str()** function, and a **String** converted to a number with the **Val()** function.
- The **Private** and **Dim** keywords allow local scope – where the variable is only accessible within a procedure or module.
- The **Public** keyword allows global scope – where the variable is accessible across an entire program.
- A variable array stores values in elements numbered from zero.
- Operators are used to perform arithmetic and comparison.
- Code can be made to conditionally branch using **If Else** statements or **Select Case** statements.
- **For Next**, **Do Until** and **Do While** statements perform code loops.
- Object properties and methods can be addressed in code.
- A **Function** returns a value but a **Sub** does not.
- Values can be sent to a **Sub** routine or a **Function** if they are of the correct data type, and of the number specified.
- The **Math** object provides many useful methods for performing mathematical calculations.
- Pseudo random numbers can be generated by the **Rnd()** function, when seeded by the **Randomize()** function.

5 Building an application

This chapter brings together elements from previous chapters to build a complete application – from the initial planning stage to its final deployment.

The program plan

When creating a new application it is useful to spend some time planning its design. Clearly define the program's precise purpose, decide what application functionality will be required, then decide what interface components will be needed.

A plan for a simple application to pick numbers for a lottery entry might look like this:

Beware

Omission of the planning stage can require time-consuming changes to be made later. It's better to "plan your work, then work your plan".

Program purpose

- The program will generate a series of six different random numbers in the range 1-59, and have the ability to be reset.

Functionality required

- An initial call to start the random number generator.
- A routine to generate and display six different random numbers.
- A routine to clear the last series from display.

Components needed

Hot tip

Toggle the value of a Button's **Enabled** property to steer the user. In this case, the application must be reset before a further series of numbers can be generated.

- Six **Label** controls to display the series of numbers – one number per Label.
- One **Button** control to generate and display the numbers in the Label controls when this Button is clicked. This Button will not be enabled when numbers are on display.
- One **Button** control to clear the numbers on display in the Label controls when this Button is clicked. This Button will not be enabled when there are no numbers on display.
- One **PictureBox** control to display a static image – just to enhance the appearance of the interface.

...cont'd

Having established a program plan means you can now create the application basics by adding the components needed to a Form.

1 Open the Visual Studio IDE and create a new Visual Basic **Windows Forms Application** project called "Lotto"

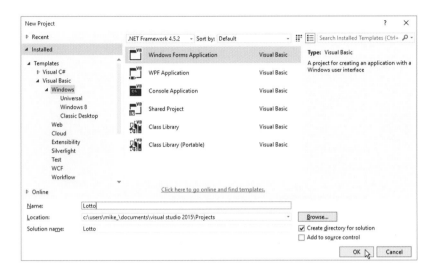

2 In the **Form Designer**, add six **Label** controls to the Form from the **Toolbox**

3 Now, add two **Button** controls and a **PictureBox** control to the Form

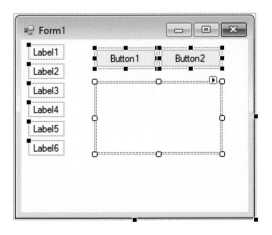

You can drag and drop items from the **Toolbox** or double-click them to add them to the Form.

Assigning static properties

Having created the application basics on the previous page, you can now assign static values using the **Properties** window.

You can open the **Properties** window using the **F4** key, or by clicking **View**, **Properties Window** on the menu bar.

1 Click anywhere on the Form to select it, then in the **Properties** window, set the Form's **Text** property to "Lotto Number Picker"

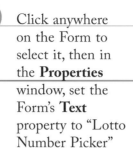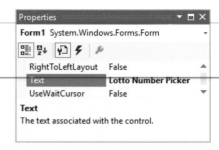

2 Select the first **Button** control, then in the **Properties** window, change its **(Name)** property to **PickBtn** and its **Text** property to "Get My Lucky Numbers"

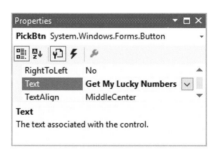

The Label controls in this program will have their Text property values assigned dynamically at runtime – so no static properties are required.

3 Select the second **Button** control, then in the **Properties** window, change its **(Name)** property to **ResetBtn** and its **Text** property to "Reset"

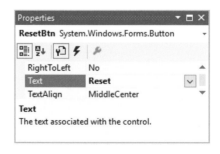

...cont'd

4 Select the **PictureBox** control, then in the **Properties**
window, click the **Image** property ellipsis button to
launch the **Select Resource** dialog

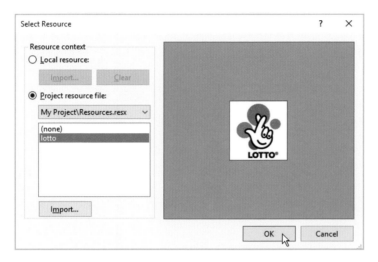

Hot tip

You can use the drop-
down list at the top of
the **Properties** window
to select any control.

5 Click the **Import** button, browse to the image location,
then click **OK** to import the image resource – this action
automatically assigns it to the PictureBox's **Image** property

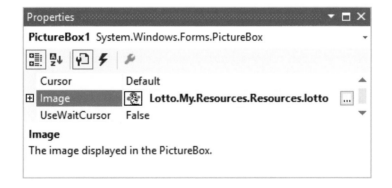

Beware

Remember to save your
project periodically as
you build it, using **File**,
Save All on the menu
bar or **Ctrl + Shift + S**
keys.

Designing the interface

Having assigned static property values on the previous page, you can now design the interface layout.

The size of both the **PictureBox** control and the **PickBtn** control first needs to be adjusted to accommodate their content. This can easily be achieved by specifying an **AutoSize** value so that Visual Basic will automatically fit the control neatly around its content.

Alternatively, you can use the **Smart Tag** arrow button on a **PictureBox** control to set its **SizeMode** property.

1. Select the **PictureBox** control, then in the **Properties** window, change its **SizeMode** property to **AutoSize**

2. Select the **PickBtn** control, then in the **Properties** window, set its **AutoSize** property to **True**

Now, you can use the Form Designer's **Format** menu and **Snap Lines** to arrange the interface components to your liking.

3. Hold down the left mouse button and drag around the Labels to select all **Label** controls

Ensure that all PictureBox **Margin** properties are set to zero, if you do not require margins around the image.

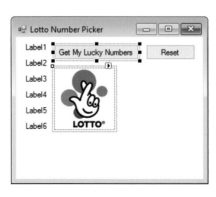

4 Click **Format, Align Tops** on the menu bar to stack the Labels into a pile

5 Click **Format, Horizontal Spacing, Make Equal** to arrange the pile of Labels into a row

In this case, it does not matter in what order the Labels appear in the row.

6 Use the Form's right grab handle to extend its width to accommodate the row of Labels and PictureBox, then drag the row and both Buttons to the top right of the Form

7 Drag the **PictureBox** control to the top left of the Form, then use the Form's bottom grab handle to adjust its height to match that of the image

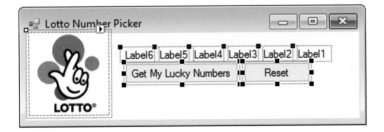

8 Use the **Snap Lines** that appear when you drag controls around the Form to position the row of Labels and the Buttons to make the interface look like this:

Set the Form's **MaximizeBox** property to **False** if you do not wish to have **Maximize** and **Minimize** buttons on the interface.

Initializing dynamic properties

Having designed the interface on the previous page, you can now add some functionality to dynamically set the initial **Text** properties of the **Label** controls and the initial **Button** states.

1 Click **View, Code** on the menu bar to open the **Code Editor** window

2 Type the following code into the declarations section then hit the **Enter** key
Private Sub Clear

The Visual Studio IDE recognizes that you want to create a new subroutine called **Clear**. It automatically adds parameter parentheses after the **Sub** name and an **End Sub** line to create a subroutine code block.

3 With the cursor inside the new subroutine code block, press **Ctrl + J** to open the **IntelliSense** pop-up window

4 Scroll down the list of items in the **IntelliSense** window and double-click on the "Label1" item to add it into the **Clear** subroutine code block

The technique described here demonstrates how to use **IntelliSense** – but you can, of course, just type the code directly.

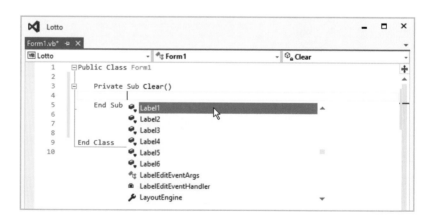

5 Type a period, then double-click the "Text" item when the **IntelliSense** window reappears to add that code

…cont'd

6 Now, type = "..." to complete the line so it reads
Label1.Text = "..."

7 Repeat this procedure for the other **Label** controls – so that the **Clear** subroutine assigns each an ellipsis string

8 With the cursor inside the **Clear** subroutine code block, use **IntelliSense** in the same way to add these two lines
PickBtn.Enabled = True
ResetBtn.Enabled = False

This completes the **Clear** subroutine functionality by setting the **Button** states. All that remains is to add a call to the **Clear** subroutine to execute all its instructions when the program starts.

9 In the **Form Designer**, double-click on the Form to open the **Code Editor** in its **Load** event-handler, then press **Ctrl + J** to open the **IntelliSense** window

10 Scroll down the list in the **IntelliSense** window and double-click on the "Clear" item you have just created

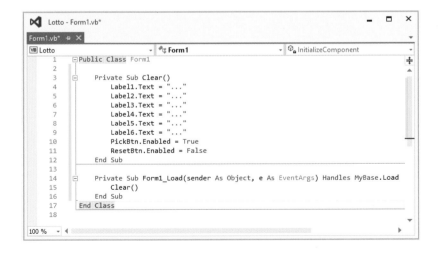

Add some line breaks and comments to make the code more friendly.

Adding runtime functionality

Having created code to initialize dynamic properties on the previous page, you can now add runtime functionality to respond to clicks on the **Button** controls.

1 In the **Form Designer**, double-click on the **ResetBtn** **Button** control to open the **Code Editor** in its **Click** event-handler, then add this call to the subroutine **Clear()**

This is all that is needed to provide dynamic functionality for the **ResetBtn** control. The main dynamic functionality of this application is provided by the **PickBtn** control, which requires the random number generator to be started when the program starts.

2 In the **Form Designer**, double-click on the Form to open the **Code Editor** in its **Load** event-handler, then add this code to start the random number generator
Randomize()

Now, you can create the code to provide dynamic functionality for the **PickBtn** control itself.

3 In the **Form Designer**, double-click on the **PickBtn** **Button** control to open the **Code Editor** in its **Click** event-handler, then add this line to declare some variables
Dim i, r, temp, nums(60) As Integer

4 Add a loop to fill the **nums** array elements 1-59 with the integer values 1 to 59
```
For i = 1 To 59
        nums(i) = i
Next
```

5 Add a second loop to shuffle the values within **nums** elements 1-59 – an algorithm to randomize their order
```
For i = 1 To 59
        r = Int(59 * Rnd()) + 1
        temp = nums(i)
        nums(i) = nums(r)
        nums(r) = temp
Next
```

Don't forget

You don't need to understand in detail the algorithm that is used to shuffle the values.

6 Now, add the following lines to display the integer values contained in **nums** elements 1-6 in the **Label** controls
```
Label1.Text = nums(1)
Label2.Text = nums(2)
Label3.Text = nums(3)
Label4.Text = nums(4)
Label5.Text = nums(5)
Label6.Text = nums(6)
```

7 Finally, add these two lines to set the **Button** states ready to reset the application
```
PickBtn.Enabled = False
ResetBtn.Enabled = True
```

Beware

The variable declaration creates integer variables called "i", "r", and "temp", along with an integer array called "nums" of 60 elements. Element **nums(0)** is not actually used though.

```
Lotto - Form1.vb                                                     _  □  ×
Form1.vb ⊕ ×
VB Lotto              ▾  ●₊ PickBtn              ▾  ⚡ Click              ▾
    19  □      Private Sub PickBtn_Click(sender As Object, e As EventArgs) ⊹
    20
    21              'Declare working variables.
    22              Dim i, r, temp, nums(60) As Integer
    23
    24              ' Fill elements 1-59 with integers 1 to 59.
    25              For i = 1 To 59
    26                  nums(i) = i
    27              Next
    28
    29              ' Shuffle the values in elements 1-59.
    30              For i = 1 To 59
    31                  r = Int(59 * Rnd()) + 1
    32                  temp = nums(i)
    33                  nums(i) = nums(r)
    34                  nums(r) = temp
    35              Next
    36
    37              ' Display the values in elements 1-6.
    38              Label1.Text = nums(1)
    39              Label2.Text = nums(2)
    40              Label3.Text = nums(3)
    41              Label4.Text = nums(4)
    42              Label5.Text = nums(5)
    43              Label6.Text = nums(6)
    44
    45              ' Set the Button states to Done.
    46              PickBtn.Enabled = False
    47              ResetBtn.Enabled = True
    48
    49          End Sub
100 %  ▾ ◀                                                            ▶
```

Hot tip

Add comments and line breaks like these to clarify the intention of your code when read by someone else – or when you revisit the code later.

Testing the program

Having worked through the program plan on the previous pages, the components needed and functionality required have now been added to the application – so it's ready to be tested.

 Click the **Start** button to run the application and examine its initial start-up appearance

The Form's **Load** event-handler has set the initial dynamic values of each **Label** control and disabled the reset button as required.

 Click the **PickBtn Button** control to execute the instructions within its **Click** event-handler

A series of numbers within the desired range is displayed and the **Button** states have changed as required – a further series of numbers cannot be generated until the application has been reset.

Hot tip

Notice that no number is repeated in any series.

3 Make a note of the numbers generated in this first series for comparison later

4 Click the **ResetBtn** control to execute the instructions within that **Click** event-handler and see the application return to its initial start-up appearance as required

5 Click the **PickBtn Button** control again to execute its **Click** event-handler code a second time

Another series of numbers within the desired range is displayed, and are different from those in the first series when compared – good, the numbers are being randomized as required.

6 Click the **Stop Debugging** button then the **Start** button to restart the application, and then click the **PickBtn Button** control once more

The generated numbers in this first series of numbers are different from those noted in the first series the last time the application ran – great, the random number generator is not repeating the same sequence of number series each time the application runs.

Failing to call the **Randomize()** method to seed the Random Number Generator will cause the application to repeat the same sequence each time it runs.

Deploying the application

Having satisfactorily tested the application on the previous page, you can now create a stand-alone version that can be executed outside the Visual Studio IDE and distributed to others for deployment elsewhere.

1 Click **Project** on the menu bar, choose **Lotto Properties**, **Signing** then select a signature certificate or simply uncheck the **Sign the ClickOnce manifests** box

2 Click **Build**, **Build Lotto**, then click **Build**, **Publish Lotto** to launch the **Publish Wizard** dialog

3 Use the wizard's **Browse** button to select a location where you wish to publish the application – the chosen location shown here is the root directory of removable drive **F:**

4 Click the **Next** button, then select whether the user will install the application from a website, network, or portable media such as CD, DVD, or removable drive – in this case, accept the default portable media option

5 Click the **Next** button, then select whether the installer should check for application updates – accept the default option not to check for updates in this case

6 Click the **Next** button to move to the final dialog page, confirm the listed choices, then click the **Finish** button to publish the application at the specified location

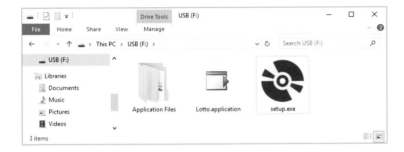

Each time you publish an application, its version number is automatically incremented – 1.0.0.0, 1.0.0.1, 1.0.0.2, etc.

The **Publish Wizard** generates a number of files including a familiar "setup.exe" executable installer.

7 Move the portable media to the system where it is to be deployed, then run **setup.exe** to install the application

When the application is installed on the client system, a shortcut is automatically added to the **Start Menu** which can be used to launch the application. The user can then run the release version of the application, just as it performed during testing of its debug version in the Visual Studio IDE.

An application cannot be published unless it has been built first.

The installer also adds an item to the client system's **Add/Remove Programs** list which can be used to uninstall the application – just like any other Windows program.

Summary

- Always make an initial program plan to avoid the need for time-consuming changes later.
- A program plan should clearly define the program purpose, functionality required, and components needed.
- Static properties, that will not change when the application is running, can be set at designtime in the **Properties** Window.
- An **AutoSize** property value makes Visual Basic automatically fit a control neatly around its content.
- The Form Designer's **Format** menu contains useful features to quickly align and space multiple interface controls.
- **Snap Lines** help you to easily align a selected control to others in the interface at designtime.
- Dynamic properties, that will change when the application is running, can be initialized with the Form's **Load** event-handler.
- The pop-up **IntelliSense** window lets you easily add program code when using the **Code Editor**.
- Runtime functionality responds to user actions by changing dynamic properties.
- A **Debug** version of an application allows its functionality to be tested as the application is being created in text format.
- The **Build** process compiles a **Release** version of an application in binary format.
- The **Publish** process creates a final **Release** version with an installer, so the application can be deployed elsewhere.
- Applications created with the Visual Studio IDE can be installed and uninstalled just like other Windows applications.

6 Solving problems

This chapter describes how to fix errors, debug code, handle exceptions, and get assistance from the Visual Studio Help system.

Real-time error detection

As you type code in the **Code Editor** window, the Visual Studio IDE is constantly monitoring your code for possible errors. When you hit the **Enter** key at the end of each line, it examines the line you have just typed and provides real-time feedback of possible errors by adding a wavy underline to any questionable code.

Warnings of potential problems are indicated by a green wavy underline. These are not critical and will not prevent execution of the application. A rollover **Tooltip** explains the warning.

1 In the **Code Editor**, type the following variable declaration in a subroutine block, then hit **Enter**
Dim num As Integer

2 A wavy green line appears below the **num** variable name. Place the cursor over the green wavy underline to discover that the warning is merely indicating a potential problem, as the variable has not yet been assigned a value

```
Private Sub routine()

    Dim num As Integer
                 (local variable) num As Integer

                 Unused local variable: 'num'.

End Sub
```

Errors are indicated by a red wavy underline. Unlike warnings, these are critical and will prevent execution of the application. A rollover **Tooltip** explains the error.

1 In the **Code Editor**, type the following variable declaration in a subroutine block, then hit **Enter**
Dim num As Integer =

2 Place the cursor over the red wavy underline to discover that the error is due to a missing value in the expression

```
Dim num As Integer =
                        Expression expected.
```

Don't forget

Warnings can be ignored but errors must be corrected.

Real-time error detection in the Visual Studio IDE is a fantastic tool to help prevent errors when you are writing code. It not only indicates errors, but can even provide a list of correction options.

1 In the **Code Editor**, type the following variable declaration in a subroutine block, then hit **Enter**
```
Dim num As Integr
```

2 A wavy red line appears below the **Integr** variable type. Place the cursor over the red wavy underline to discover that the error is due to an unknown type specification

3 Click the lightbulb icon or click the **Show potential fixes** link to see a list of error correction options

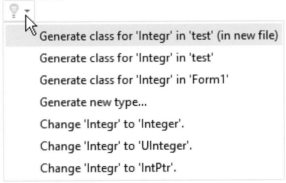

4 If this error is simply a spelling error for the **Integer** data type, select the option to **Change 'Integr' to 'Integer'** to see your code get instantly corrected accordingly

Visual Studio 2015 provides live code analysis that displays a light bulb when the compiler detects an issue with your code, and has a suggestion of how to fix that issue.

Hot tip

Other correction options enable you to create a new data type, if that is what you require.

Fixing compile errors

While syntax errors, like those on the previous page, can be detected by the **Code Editor** in real-time, other errors that employ correct syntax cannot be detected until the code is compiled. Compile errors are typically errors of logic, and they cause the execution to halt when an "exception" occurs. For example, when incompatible data types appear in an expression, an **InvalidCastException** occurs and execution stops immediately.

1 In the **Code Editor**, type the following lines into a subroutine code block
```
Dim num As Double = 7.5
Dim str As String = "five"
MsgBox( num * str )
```

2 Click the **Start** button to run the subroutine and see execution is soon halted. The line causing the exception becomes highlighted in the **Code Editor**, and an **Exception Assistant** pop-up window appears with a list of possible solutions

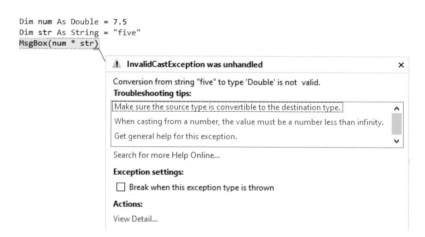

Hot tip

You can click on the **View Details** link in the Exception Assistant's **Actions** list for more error information.

To fix this **InvalidCastException**, the code would obviously need amending so both expression values are of the **Double** data type.

The cause of other compile errors may be less obvious without some further investigation. For example, when a loop that is reading array elements attempts to address an element index that does not exist, causing an **IndexOutOfRangeException**.

...cont'd

Execution halts immediately, so it is useful to examine the counter value to identify the precise iteration causing the compile error.

1 In the **Code Editor**, type the following variable declaration and loop into a subroutine code block

```
Dim i, nums(10) As Integer
For i = 1 to 20
        nums(i) = i
Next
```

2 Click the **Start** button to run the subroutine and see execution is soon halted. The code causing the exception becomes highlighted in the **Code Editor** and an **Exception Assistant** pop-up window appears with a list of possible solutions

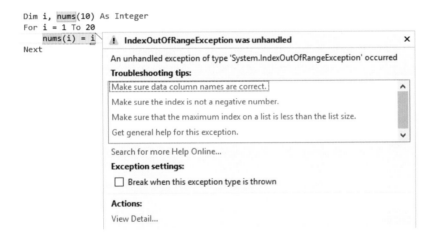

```
Dim i, nums(10) As Integer
For i = 1 To 20
    nums(i) = i
Next
```

⚠ **IndexOutOfRangeException was unhandled** ✕

An unhandled exception of type 'System.IndexOutOfRangeException' occurred

Troubleshooting tips:

Make sure data column names are correct.

Make sure the index is not a negative number.

Make sure that the maximum index on a list is less than the list size.

Get general help for this exception.

Search for more Help Online...

Exception settings:

☐ Break when this exception type is thrown

Actions:

View Detail...

3 Place the cursor over the counter variable to see a pop-up appear, showing its current value

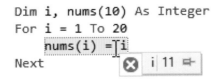

```
Dim i, nums(10) As Integer
For i = 1 To 20
    nums(i) = i
Next
```
❌ i 11 ⇥

It's now clear that execution halted when the loop attempted to address **nums(11)** – beyond the bounds of last element **nums(10)**. To fix this **IndexOutOfRangeException**, the code would need amending to end the loop after 10 iterations.

Beware

Another common compile error is the **FileNotFoundException**, which occurs when a file is missing or its path name is incorrect.

Debugging code

It is sometimes useful to closely examine the progression of a program by watching its execution line by line, to locate any bugs. Progress is controlled by clicking the ⁑ **Step Into** button on the **Debug** menu bar to move through the program one line at a time. When you begin debugging, you can open a **Watch** window to monitor the value of particular variables as execution proceeds.

Hot tip

If you can't see the **Step Into** button, right-click on the menu bar and select **Debug** to add the debugging buttons there.

1 Double-click on a Form to open the **Code Editor** in its **Load** event-handler, then add the following code
```
Dim i As Integer
Dim pass As Integer = 0
Dim base As Integer = 2
For i = 1 To 2
        pass = pass + 1
        base = Square( base )
Next
```

2 Now, add this arithmetic function into the declarations section of the code with these lines
```
Function Square(ByVal num As Integer)
        num = num * num
        Return num
End Function
```

3 In the **Code Editor**, click in the gray margin against the **Load** event-handler – to set a debug starting "breakpoint"

```
Private Sub Form1_Load(sender As Object, e As EventArgs) Handles MyBase.Load
```

4 Click the **Step Into** button once to begin debugging

Don't forget

You can click the **Stop Debugging** button at any time, to return to normal **Code Editor** mode.

5 Click **Debug**, **Windows**, **Watch**, **Watch1** on the menu bar to launch a **Watch** window

6 Type the variable name "pass" into the **Name** column and hit **Enter**, then repeat to add the "base" variable name

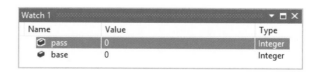

Watch 1		▼ □ ×
Name	Value	Type
☑ pass	0	Integer
☑ base	0	Integer

7 Click **Step Into** five times to reach the **Square** function call in the first loop iteration, and note the variable values

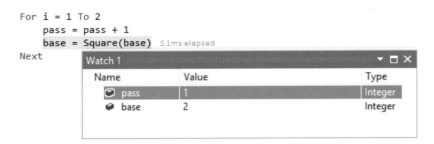

```
For i = 1 To 2
    pass = pass + 1
    base = Square(base)   ≤1ms elapsed
Next
```

Name	Value	Type
pass	1	Integer
base	2	Integer

8 Click **Step Into** eight more times to progress through each line of the **Square** function and the loop, returning to the function call on the second iteration

```
For i = 1 To 2
    pass = pass + 1
    base = Square(base)   ≤1ms elapsed
Next
```

Name	Value	Type
pass	2	Integer
base	4	Integer

9 Click the **Step Over** button once to execute the function, without stepping through each line

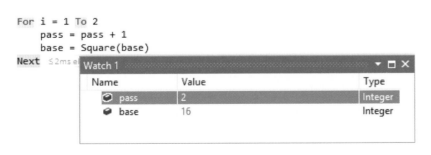

```
For i = 1 To 2
    pass = pass + 1
    base = Square(base)
Next  ≤2ms e
```

Name	Value	Type
pass	2	Integer
base	16	Integer

Hot tip

The **Step Out** button is used to return to the function caller when you are stepping through lines of a called function.

10 When you have finished debugging, click the red dot you added in the margin to remove the breakpoint

Setting debug breakpoints

In all but the smallest of programs, stepping through each line is very tedious when debugging. Instead, you can quickly reach the part you wish to examine by setting a "breakpoint" to halt execution on a particular line. Setting one or more breakpoints is useful to help you understand how certain Visual Basic code constructs work – such as the nested loop construct shown here:

1 Double-click on a Form to open the **Code Editor** in its **Load** event-handler, and type this code

```
Dim i, j, k As Integer
Dim pass As Integer = 0
For i = 1 To 3
        For j = 1 To 3
                For k = 1 To 3
                        pass = pass + 1
                Next
        Next
Next
```

2 In the **Code Editor**, click in the gray margin against each line containing the **Next** keyword, to set three breakpoints – a red dot will appear in the margin and each **Next** statement is highlighted to indicate the set breakpoints

3 Click the **Start** button and see the application run to the first breakpoint it meets

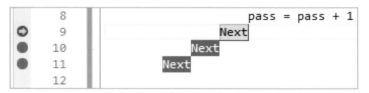

4 Click **Debug, Windows, Locals** to launch the **Locals** window to follow the current value of each variable

Yellow arrows indicate the current position. Click on the red dot to cancel a breakpoint.

...cont'd

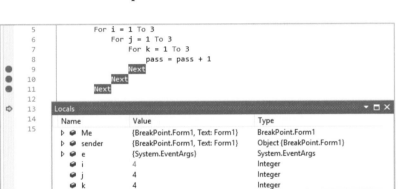

Name	Value	Type
▷ ● Me	{BreakPoint.Form1, Text: Form1}	BreakPoint.Form1
▷ ● sender	{BreakPoint.Form1, Text: Form1}	Object {BreakPoint.Form1}
▷ ● e	{System.EventArgs}	System.EventArgs
● i	1	Integer
● j	1	Integer
● k	1	Integer
● pass	1	Integer

5 Watch the variable values change as you repeatedly click the **Start** (**Continue**) button to move to each **Next** breakpoint until you reach the third outer **Next** statement, then click **Step Into** to reach the end of the subroutine

The **Locals** window shows all variables in current scope as the program proceeds.

```
 5          For i = 1 To 3
 6              For j = 1 To 3
 7                  For k = 1 To 3
 8                      pass = pass + 1
 9              Next
10          Next
11      Next
12
13
14
15
```

Name	Value	Type
▷ ● Me	{BreakPoint.Form1, Text: Form1}	BreakPoint.Form1
▷ ● sender	{BreakPoint.Form1, Text: Form1}	Object {BreakPoint.Form1}
▷ ● e	{System.EventArgs}	System.EventArgs
● i	4	Integer
● j	4	Integer
● k	4	Integer
● pass	27	Integer

At the end of the subroutine, each counter variable has been incremented beyond the upper limit set in the **For** statements, to exit each loop. There have been a total of 27 iterations (3x3x3).

6 Click **Stop Debugging** to finish, then click the **Start** button to once more run to the first breakpoint

7 Click **Debug**, **Windows**, **Immediate** to launch the **Immediate** window

8 In the **Immediate** window type i = 3 and hit **Enter**, then use the **Step Into** button to step through each line of the final complete outer loop iteration

Any code you type into the **Immediate** window is dynamically applied to the application being debugged, but does not change its code. Try typing **MsgBox("Hi")** into the **Immediate** window, then hit the **Enter** key.

103

Detecting runtime errors

While the **Code Editor** provides real-time detection of syntax errors, and the compiler provides detection of logic errors, it is the responsibility of the programmer to anticipate user actions that may cause runtime errors when the application is in use. Consideration of all the different ways a user could employ your application is important to predict potential runtime errors.

1 In a new project add **Label**, **TextBox**, and **Button** controls to a Form, so it looks like this:

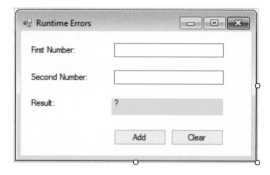

2 Name the yellow **Label** "ResultLbl"

3 Double-click on the "Add" button to open the **Code Editor** in its **Click** event-handler, then type the code below to create a simple adding machine
```
Dim num1 As Integer = Val( TextBox1.Text )
Dim num2 As Integer = Val( TextBox2.Text )
ResultLbl.Text = num1 + num2
```

4 Enter numeric values into each text field, then click the "Add" button to see the application perform as expected

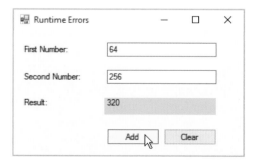

Adding floating point values with this application will produce a result rounded to the nearest integer.

...cont'd

5 Now, try adding large numbers like those shown here – an error will occur and the system will halt the program, complaining of an overflow

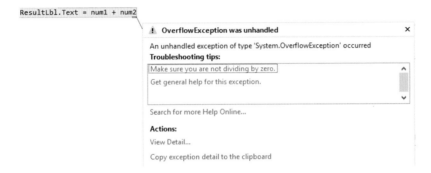

While the programmer may not have intended the application to be used to add such large numbers, it is possible the user may wish to do so – and this possibility should have been considered in order to predict this type of runtime error. The overflow has, in fact, occurred because the **Integer** data type can only store numeric values up to around two billion. This problem can be fixed by changing the variables to use a **Long** data type instead.

6 Quit the application then edit the "Add" button's **Click** event-handler to read like this:
```
Dim num1 As Long = Val( TextBox1.Text )
Dim num2 As Long = Val( TextBox2.Text )
ResultLbl.Text = num1 + num2
```

The precise value range of the **Integer** data type is -2,147,483,648 through 2,147,483,647.

7 Save the amended project, then run the application and try again to add the two long numbers

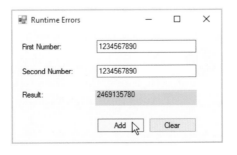

105

Catching runtime errors

When you are able to predict potential runtime errors by considering all eventualities, you can provide code to handle exceptions that may arise with a **Try Catch** code block. Your program can supply information to the user about the error, should you wish to do so, then proceed normally. This technique could be used to provide code to handle the exception that arose in the previous example, instead of the fix suggested.

1 Repeat steps 1, 2 and 3 on page 104 to recreate the simple adding machine application, then click the **Start** button to run the application in **Debug** mode

2 Enter two long numbers, then click the "Add" button to attempt the addition – the compiler reports that an **OverflowException** has occurred

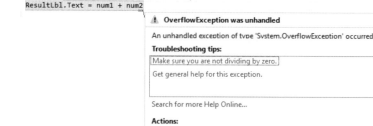

Hot tip

You can use the right-click context menu to quickly switch between the **Code Editor** and the **Form Designer**.

3 Click the **Stop Debugging** button so you can edit the code

4 Right-click in the "Add" button's **Click** event-handler code block, then choose **Insert Snippet**, **Code Patterns**, **Error Handling (Exceptions)** from the context menu

5 Double-click **Try...Catch...End Try Statement** to paste a **Try Catch** code block into the **Code Editor**

```
- If, For Each, Try Catch, Property, etc  >  Error Handling (Exceptions)  >
                                                 Define An Exception Class
                                                 Throw an Exception
                                                 Try...Catch...End Try Statement
                                                 Try...Catch...Finally...End Try Statement
                                                 Try...Finally...End Try Statement
                                                 Using Statement
```

```
Dim Try

Catch ex As ArgumentException

End Try
```

Insert Snippet contains lots of useful pieces of code to paste into the **Code Editor** – take some time to explore its contents.

6 Type "OverflowException" in place of **ArgumentException** in the pasted code block

7 Cut and paste the original lines of code to put them between the **Try** and **Catch** lines

8 Add this code between the **Catch** and **End Try** lines **MsgBox("Only numbers up to 2 Billion are allowed")**

```
Try

    Dim num1 As Integer = Val(TextBox1.Text)
    Dim num2 As Integer = Val(TextBox2.Text)
    ResultLbl.Text = num1 + num2

Catch ex As OverflowException

    MsgBox("Only numbers up to 2 Billion are allowed")

End Try
```

Try adding code to handle the exceptions on page 98 and 99 instead of the suggested fixes.

9 Click the **Start** button, then enter long numbers as before and click the "Add" button, to see the exception handled

CatchErrors   ✕

Only numbers up to 2 Billion are allowed

OK

10 Click **OK** to close the **MsgBox**, then change the numbers to be within the allowed range and click the "Add" button to proceed normally

107

Getting help

The Visual Studio **Help** system provides an extensive source of reference for many programming languages. You can choose to install a Help Library on your computer for the Visual Basic programming language, so you can easily refer to it at any time:

The **Help Viewer** allows you to download **Help** libraries for offline use, check for available updates, and seek help from installed **Help** libraries.

1 On the Visual Studio menu bar, click **Help**, **Add and Remove Help Content** to open the **Help Viewer**

Help		
❓ View Help	Ctrl+F1
▦ Add and Remove Help Content	Ctrl+Alt+F1
Set Help Preference	▸

2 On the **Manage Content** tab, expand **Recommended Documentation** then choose the **Visual Basic** library

3 When your selection is added to the **Pending changes** list, click the **Update** button to download that library

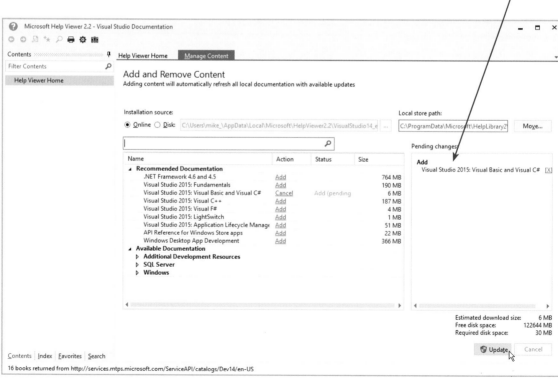

Help library documentation can be searched for answers to your Visual Basic coding questions. For example, you might need to discover all data types available in Visual Basic programming.

1 On the menu bar click **Help**, **Set Help Preference**, **Launch in Help Viewer** to use installed libraries

You can choose **Set Help Preference** to **Launch in Browser** if you want to search online help without installing libraries, but local help is often more convenient.

2 Next, click **Help**, **View Help** to launch **Help Viewer**

3 Now, enter "visual basic data types" in the **Help Viewer** Search box, then hit **Enter** to see the results

4 Finally, choose **Data Types Summary (Visual Basic)**

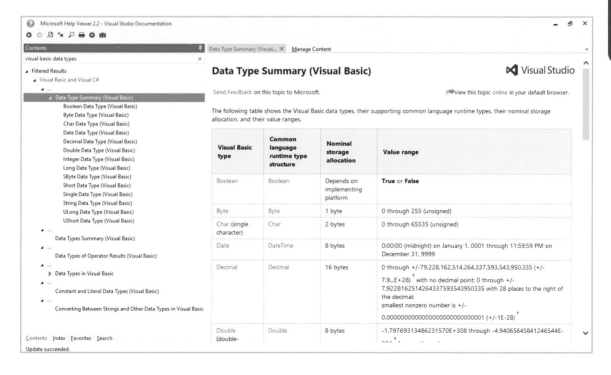

Summary

- The **Code Editor** constantly monitors your code to provide real-time error detection.
- Warnings are not critical and are indicated by a green wavy underline – whereas errors are critical, and are indicated by a red wavy underline.
- A lightbulb icon at the end of a red wavy underline indicates that a list of possible corrections is available.
- Typically, real-time errors are errors of syntax, and compile errors are errors of logic.
- When a compile error occurs in **Debug Mode**, execution stops and the **Exception Assistant** offers a list of possible fixes.
- In **Debug Mode** you can discover the current value of any variable simply by placing the cursor over the variable name.
- The **Step Into** button lets you walk through a program one line at a time.
- The **Step Over** button lets you bypass the lines of a called function, and the **Step Out** button lets you return to the line where that function is called.
- Variable values can be monitored as a program proceeds using the **Watch** window or the **Locals** window.
- Breakpoints halt the execution of a program to allow examination of the part of the program where they are set.
- In **Debug Mode**, code can be dynamically applied using the **Immediate** window.
- Runtime errors occur when the user action has not been anticipated by the programmer.
- Use a **Try Catch** block to handle anticipated exceptions.
- The **Help** library system provides extensive reference sources for both offline and online assistance.

7 Extending the interface

This chapter demonstrates how applications can incorporate dialogs, menus, multiple forms, and Windows Media Player.

Color, Font & Image dialogs

The Visual Studio IDE makes it simple to add the capability to call upon the standard Windows selection dialogs, so the user can choose options within your applications. For example, selection of colors, fonts, and images.

1 Start a new **Windows Forms Application** project and add a **PictureBox**, **TextBox**, and three **Button** controls to the Form

2 Name the **Button** controls **ColorBtn**, **FontBtn**, and **ImgBtn**

3 From the **Dialogs** section of the **Toolbox**, add a **ColorDialog**, **FontDialog**, and **OpenFileDialog** component to the Form – see them appear in the **Component Tray** at the bottom of the Form Designer

ColorDialog1   FontDialog1   OpenFileDialog1

4 Double-click the **ColorBtn Button** and add this code to its **Click** event-handler
```
If ColorDialog1.ShowDialog = DialogResult.OK Then
        Me.BackColor = ColorDialog1.Color
End If
```

5 Double-click the **FontBtn Button** and add this code to its **Click** event-handler
```
If FontDialog1.ShowDialog = DialogResult.OK Then
        TextBox1.Font = FontDialog1.Font
End If
```

Set the TextBox's **Multiline** property to **True** so you can make it taller than a regular single line.

6 Double-click the **ImgBtn Button** and add this code to its **Click** event-handler

```
If OpenFileDialog1.ShowDialog = DialogResult.OK Then
  Try
        PictureBox1.Image = _
        New Bitmap(OpenFileDialog1.FileName)
  Catch ex As ArgumentException
        MsgBox("Not an image")
  End Try
End If
```

7 Click the **Start** button to run the application, then click the **ColorBtn Button** to launch the familiar Windows **Color** selection dialog

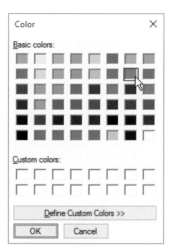

8 Choose a color then click the **OK** button to apply it to the Form's background

The **OpenFileDialog** allows the user to select any file. The **Try Catch** statement handles the **ArgumentException** that is thrown if the user chooses a file type that is not an image.

9 Type some text in the **TextBox**, then click the **FontBtn Button** and choose a Font for that text

10 Click the **ImgBtn Button**, then browse to select an image to assign to the **PictureBox** control

Open, Save & Print dialogs

Applications created with Visual Basic can call upon the standard Windows selection dialogs to allow the user to open, save and print files.

1 Start a new **Windows Forms Application** and add a **RichTextBox** and three **Button** controls to the Form – name the **Button** controls **OpenBtn**, **SaveBtn**, and **PrintBtn**

2 From the **Dialogs** section of the Toolbox, add an **OpenFileDialog** and **SaveFileDialog** component, then add a **PrintDialog** component from the **Printing** section of the Toolbox – see them appear in the **Component Tray** at the bottom of the Form Designer

OpenFileDialog1   SaveFileDialog1   PrintDialog1

3 Double-click the **OpenBtn Button** and add this code to its **Click** event-handler

```
With OpenFileDialog1
        .Title = "Open File"
        .Filter = "Rich Text Files | *.rtf"
        .FileName = ""
        .CheckFileExists = vbTrue
End With

If OpenFileDialog1.ShowDialog = DialogResult.OK Then
RichTextBox1.LoadFile(OpenFileDialog1.FileName, _
        RichTextBoxStreamType.RichText)
End If
```

Hot tip

Always define filter options to determine which file types the **OpenFileDialog** can see.

4 Double-click the **PrintBtn Button** and add this code to its **Click** event-handler

```
If PrintDialog1.ShowDialog = _
        Windows.Forms.DialogResult.OK Then
        ' Insert code here to process and print.
End If
```

5 Double-click the **SaveBtn** Button and add this code to its
Click event-handler

```
With SaveFileDialog1
        .Title = "Save File"
        .Filter = "Rich Text Files | *.rtf"
        .DefaultExt = ".rtf"
        .OverWritePrompt = True
End With

If SaveFileDialog1.ShowDialog = DialogResult.OK Then
RichTextBox1.SaveFile(SaveFileDialog1.FileName, _
        RichTextBoxStreamType.RichText)
End If
```

6 Click the **Start** button to run the app, then use the
OpenBtn Button to launch the familiar Windows **Open
File** dialog

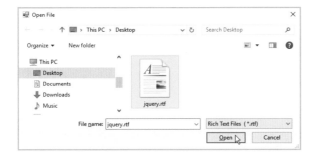

7 Choose a Rich Text File (**.rtf**) on your computer, then
click **Open** to load it in the **RichTextBox** control

8 Click the **SaveBtn
Button** to launch
the familiar **Save
File** dialog, and save
the loaded file with
a different name

9 Click the **PrintBtn Button** to launch the familiar
Windows **Print** dialog, where you can select **Printer
preferences** before printing

The **Print** dialog does
not automatically
know how to print the
document – you need to
provide code to enable
printing. See page
151 for an example of
how to print plain text
documents.

Creating application menus

Drop-down menus, toolbars, and status bars, like those found in most Windows applications, can easily be added to your own Visual Basic applications from the Toolbox.

1 Find the **Menus & Toolbars** section of the **Toolbox**, then double-click the **MenuStrip** item to add it to the Form

2 Click the **MenuStrip** control's arrow button on its **Smart Tag**, then select the option to **Insert Standard Items**

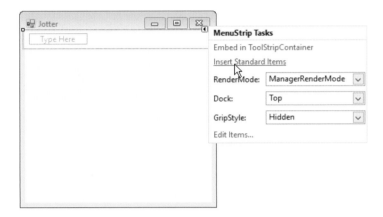

3 When the familiar headings and items have been added to the **MenuStrip**, right-click on any item and use the context menu to edit that item. You can also type new custom items into the **Type Here** boxes as required

You can create your own custom menus using the **Type Here** boxes instead of **Insert Standard Items**.

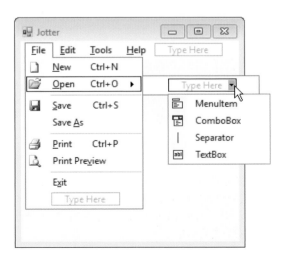

4 In the **Toolbox**, double-click on the **ToolStrip** item to add it to the Form, then click its **Smart Tag** button and once more select **Insert Standard Items**

5 When the familiar icon buttons have been added to the **ToolStrip**, right-click on any item and use the context menu to edit that item. Also, add further custom items from the drop-down list as required

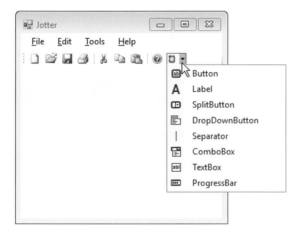

6 In the **Toolbox**, double-click on the **StatusStrip** item to add it to the Form

7 Select the **StatusLabel** item from the **StatusStrip** drop-down list, then set its text property to "Ready"

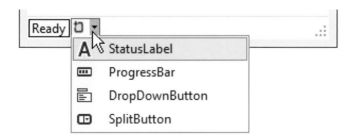

Use **StatusBar** messages to provide feedback to the user.

8 Add a **RichTextBox** control to the center of the Form, click its **Smart Tag** button and select the option to **Dock in parent container**, then ensure that its **ScrollBars** property is set to **Both**

Making menus work

The menu items and toolbar buttons created on the previous page will not perform their desired actions until you add some code to make them work. For actions that feature both in a menu and on a toolbar button, it is best to create a subroutine that can be called from the menu item's **Click** event-handler and the button's **Click** event-handler – to avoid duplication.

Be careful not to double-click on the menu item's name unless you want to edit the default keyboard shortcut – click at the side of the name to open the **Code Editor**.

1 In Form Designer, click **File, New** to select the **New** menu item

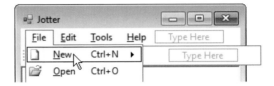

2 Double-click on the **New** menu item to open the **Code Editor** in its event-handler, and add this call
NewFile()

3 Immediately below the **End Sub** line of the **New** menu item's event-handler, add this custom subroutine
Private Sub NewFile()
RichTextBox1.Text = ""
ToolStripStatusLabel1.Text = "Ready"
End Sub

4 Return to the **Form Designer**, then double-click on the **New** toolbar button to open the **Code Editor** in that event-handler, and add a call to the custom subroutine
NewFile()

5 Add an **OpenFileDialog** and **SaveFileDialog** component from the **Dialogs** section of the **Toolbox**

6 In the **Click** event-handlers of both the **Open** menu item and the **Open** toolbar button, add this code
OpenFile()

7 Immediately below the **End Sub** line of the **Open** menu
item's event-handler, add this custom subroutine
```
Private Sub OpenFile()
OpenFileDialog1.Filter = "Text Files | *.txt"
If OpenFileDialog1.ShowDialog = _
        Windows.Forms.DialogResult.OK Then
RichTextBox1.LoadFile(OpenFileDialog1.FileName, _
        RichTextBoxStreamType.PlainText) End If
End Sub
```

8 In the **Click** event-handlers of both the **Save** menu item
and the **Save** toolbar button, add this code
```
SaveFile()
```

9 Immediately below the **End Sub** line of the **Save** menu
item's event-handler, add this custom subroutine
```
Private Sub SaveFile()
SaveFileDialog1.Filter = "Text Files | *.txt"
If SaveFileDialog1.ShowDialog = _
        Windows.Forms.DialogResult.OK Then
RichTextBox1.SaveFile(SaveFileDialog1.FileName, _
        RichTextBoxStreamType.PlainText)   End If
End Sub
```

10 Run the application and test the functionality of the **New**,
Open, and **Save** file menu items and toolbar buttons

You can add functionality to the **File**, **Exit** menu item simply by adding **Application. Exit()** to its **Click** event-handler.

Keyboard shortcuts are already configured – try **Ctrl + N**, **Ctrl + S**, and **Ctrl + O** to test them.

Adding more forms

Most Windows applications have more than one Form – even the simplest application usually has an **About** dialog, and perhaps a **Splash Screen**, to provide version information to the user. These can easily be added to your applications in Visual Basic.

You can also right-click on the project name icon in **Solution Explorer** and choose **Properties**, to open the **Project Designer**.

1 Click **Project**, **Add New Item** on the menu bar, to launch the **Add New Item** dialog, then select the **About Box** icon and click the **Add** button

2 Select **Project**, *ProjectName* **Properties** on the menu bar, to open the **Project Designer** window, then choose **Application** and click the **Assembly Information...** button

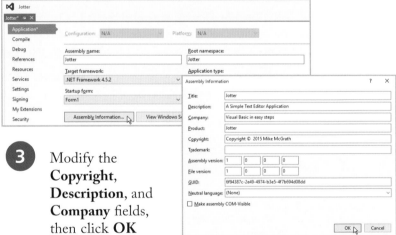

Don't forget

The descriptive information in the **Assembly Information** dialog will appear in the **About** dialog.

3 Modify the **Copyright**, **Description**, and **Company** fields, then click **OK**

4 In **Form Designer**, double-click on the **About** item in the **Help** menu then add this code to its **Click** event-handler

`AboutBox1.ShowDialog()`

5 Click the **Start** button to run the application, then click **Help**, **About** to see the **About** dialog

Adding a Splash Screen

1 Click **Project**, **Add New Item** on the menu bar to launch the **Add New Item** dialog, then select the **Splash Screen** icon and click the **Add** button

2 Click **Project**, **Properties** on the menu bar, to open the **Project Designer** window

3 Open the **Splash Screen** drop-down list at the bottom of the **Project Designer** window, and select **SplashScreen1**

4 Click the **Start** button to run the application and see a **Splash Screen** display for about two seconds before the main Form appears

The **Splash Screen** and **About** dialog are similar – both display information from the **Assembly Information**, but less detail is shown in the **Splash Screen** because it is only displayed briefly.

Controlling multiple forms

Applications sometimes need more than one Form to accommodate the user interface. When the user moves to the second Form, the first one can be hidden so any information it contains will remain in memory and reappear when the user returns to that Form. Similarly, the second Form can be hidden so any user input it contains is available to the program when the user returns to the first Form. Alternatively, the second Form can be closed when the user returns to the first Form, but any user input will then be lost unless it has been stored in variables.

1 Add two **Button** and **Label** controls to a Form so it looks like this, and name the yellow **Label ValueLbl**

2 Click **Project**, **Add New Item** and add another **Windows Form** to the project

3 Add a **TextBox** and two **Button** controls to this Form, naming the Buttons **CloseBtn** and **HideBtn**

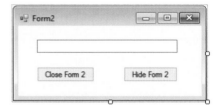

4 In **Form Designer**, double-click on the "Hide Form 1" **Button** in **Form 1** and add this code to its **Click** event-handler
```
Me.Hide()
Form2.Show()
```

5 Now, double-click on the "Show Hidden Value" **Button** in **Form 1** and add this code to that **Click** event-handler
```
ValueLbl.Text = Form2.TextBox1.Text
```

Consider using multiple Forms when the application interface becomes cluttered with many controls.

6 In **Form Designer**, double-click on the "Hide Form 2" **Button** in **Form 2** and add this code to its **Click** event-handler

Me.Hide()
Form1.Show()

7 Now, double-click on the "Close Form 2" **Button** in **Form 2** and add this code to that **Click** event-handler

Me.Close()
Form1.Show()

8 Click the **Start** button to run the application and click the "Hide Form 1" **Button** – to see that **Form 1** disappears and **Form 2** appears

9 Type something into the **TextBox** then click on the "Hide Form 2" **Button** – **Form 2** disappears, and **Form 1** reappears

10 Click the "Show Hidden Value" **Button** in **Form 1** – the text you typed into the **TextBox** in **Form 2** gets copied into the **ValueLbl** **Label** in **Form 1**

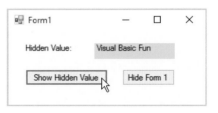

11 Click "Hide Form 1" once more, then type something else in the **TextBox** and click the "Close Form 2" **Button**

12 Click the "Show Hidden Value" **Button** in **Form 1** again – nothing is displayed in the **ValueLbl** **Label** as your input is now lost

Try creating a variable to store the value in the **TextBox** when **Form 2** gets closed so the user input can be recalled.

123

Playing sounds

Sound files can be included within an application as a resource, in much the same way that image files can be imported as a resource, to enhance the application. These can then be played, as required, by calling upon the Windows Media Player on the local system.

1 Start a new **Windows Forms Application** project and add a single **Button** control to the Form

2 Select **Project**, *ProjectName* **Properties** on the menu bar, to open the **Project Designer** window

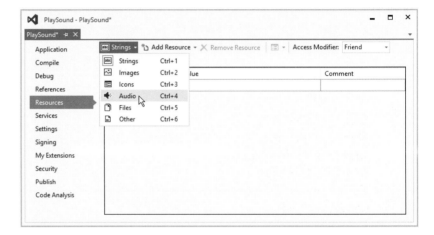

3 In **Project Designer**, select the **Resources** side tab, then the **Audio** item from the drop-down list

4 Select the **Add Existing File...** item from the **Add Resource** drop-down list to launch the **Add existing file to resources** dialog

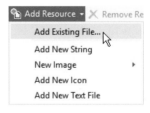

You can add an icon resource and assign it to the Form's **Icon** property in its **Load** event-handler.

5 Browse to the location of the sound file you wish to add, then click the **Add** button

...cont'd

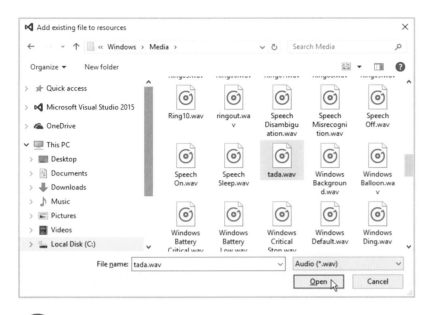

You can typically find the Windows sound files in the folder on your computer at **C:\Windows\Media**.

6 See that the sound file **tada.wav** now gets added to the **Resources** folder in **Solution Explorer** and appears in the **Resources** window of **Project Designer**

7 Click the **X** button to close the **Project Designer** and click **Yes** when asked if you want to save changes

A sound can be played repeatedly using the **PlayLooping()** method – the loop can be ended with the **Stop()** method.

8 Click **View, Code** on the menu bar to open the **Code Editor,** then add this line to the declarations section
```
Friend WithEvents player _
        As New System.Media.SoundPlayer
```

9 In **Form Designer,** double-click the **Button** then add the following code to its **Click** event-handler
```
player.Stream = My.Resources.tada
player.Play()
```

10 Click the **Start** button to run the application, then click the **Button** to play the sound

Playing multimedia

A Visual Basic application can employ an **ActiveX** instance of the Windows Media Player to play all types of local media files within the application interface.

1 Start a new **Windows Forms Application** project, then add a **Button** control to the Form and an **OpenFileDialog** component

2 In the **Toolbox**, right-click on the **Components** section and select **Choose Items** from the context menu

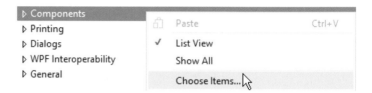

3 When the **Choose Toolbox Items** dialog appears, click its **COM Components** tab, then check "Windows Media Player" and click **OK** – a new **Windows Media Player** item gets added to the Toolbox **Components** section

The **Common Object Model (COM)** is a standard platform that allows components to be easily shared.

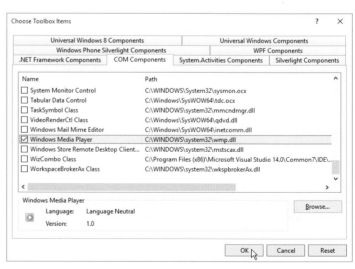

4 From the **Toolbox**, add a **Windows Media Player** component to the Form and resize it so its display and controls are fully visible – note that component is called **AxWindowsMediaPlayer1**

5 In **Form Designer**, double-click the **Button** to open the **Code Editor** in its **Click** event-handler, and add the following code

```
With OpenFileDialog1
  .Title = "Media File Browser"
  .Filter = "Media Files (*.wmv;*.mp3)|*.wmv;*.mp3"
  .FileName = ""
  .CheckFileExists = True
End With

If OpenFileDialog1.ShowDialog = DialogResult.OK Then
AxWindowsMediaPlayer1.URL = _
      OpenFileDialog1.Filename
End If
```

6 Run the application, then click the **Button** control to launch the **OpenFileDialog** and choose a valid media file – see it start playing in the application interface

Notice how multiple file formats must be separated by a semi-colon in the **Filter** statement.

Try adding a status bar to display the name of the file currently playing.

Summary

- The **Dialogs** section of the **Toolbox** contains components that can be added to an application to call upon the standard Windows dialogs to select Colors, Fonts, Images, and Files.

- **Open File** and **Save File** dialogs can be configured to filter file types so they only display files of a specified file extension.

- A **Print** dialog allows the user to select printer options but it cannot automatically print.

- Familiar menus can easily be added to an application using the **Insert Standard Items** option of the **MenuStrip** component.

- The **ToolStrip** component provides familiar toolbar icons.

- You can add a **StatusStrip** component to provide an application status bar to display feedback to the user.

- Where both **MenuStrip** and **ToolStrip** components appear in an application, it is best to create subroutines to be called when the user chooses a menu item or associated icon.

- A **MenuStrip** component automatically provides keyboard shortcuts for each of its menu items.

- The **Add New Item** option on the **Project** menu can be used to add a **Form**, **About Box** dialog, and **Splash Screen**.

- Multiple forms can be controlled using their **Show()**, **Hide()**, and **Close()** methods.

- Applications can be enhanced by including audio files in their **Resources** folder to provide sound.

- Windows **COM Components** can be added to the standard selection of components on the Visual Studio Toolbox.

- An **ActiveX** instance of Windows Media Player can be added to an interface, to allow the application to play multimedia files.

8 Scripting with Visual Basic

This chapter illustrates how Visual Basic may be used outside the Visual Studio IDE to add functionality to Microsoft Office applications, and to perform useful tasks with Windows Script Host.

Introducing VBA macros

Visual Basic for Applications (VBA) is the programming language built into Microsoft Office applications. It shares the same core Visual Basic language as that in the Visual Studio IDE, but has different available objects in each application – Word has an **ActiveDocument** object and Excel has an **ActiveSheet** object.

Where Microsoft Office is installed on a system, all Office objects are available across all versions of Visual Basic. So you can program Word from Excel, or from a standalone application created in the Visual Studio IDE.

VBA has a **Form Designer** and **Debugger** much like those in the Visual Studio IDE, but with a more limited set of features.

Form Designer

Run Button   Project Window   Properties Window

Toolbox

Code Editor

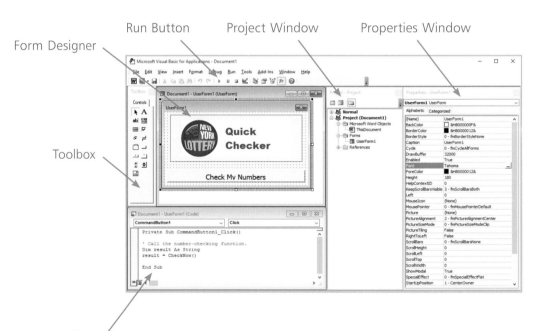

You cannot create standalone, executable applications with Visual Basic for Applications, as it has no native code compiler, but you can create a script, hidden within the document file, to execute a series of instructions upon the document. This is known as a "macro" and is typically used to automate a task you perform regularly that requires multiple commands. For example, to insert a table with a specific style and number of rows and columns.

…cont'd

1 Launch Microsoft Word, or
any other Office application,
then click the **Developer** tab
and choose the **Visual Basic**
ribbon icon to launch the
Visual Basic Editor

2 In the **Visual Basic Editor**, click **Insert**, **Module** to open
the **Code Editor** window

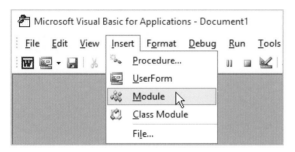

131

If the **Developer** tab
is not visible, click **File**,
Options, **Customize
Ribbon**, and check the
"Developer" box in the
Main Tabs options.

3 In the **Code Editor**, type this Visual Basic subroutine
Private Sub Hello()
  MsgBox("Hello from VBA!")
End Sub

4 In the **Visual Basic Editor**, click
the **Run** button to execute the
subroutine– the Visual Basic Editor
gets minimized until you click the
OK button in the Message Box

Our examples describe
Office 2016. For versions
of Office earlier than
Office 2007, the Visual
Basic Editor is launched
from the **Tools**, **Macros**
menu.

Creating a Word macro

Bookmarks can be inserted into a Word document to indicate the position at which a macro should insert content.

1 Open a new document in Word, type this book's title, then use **Insert**, **Links**, **Bookmark** to add a bookmark, and name it "mark"

2 Click **Developer**, **Visual Basic**, or press **Alt + F11**, to launch the **Visual Basic Editor**

3 In the **Visual Basic Editor**, click **Insert**, **Module** to open the **Code Editor** window

4 Now, type the following code into the **Code Editor**

```
Sub AddTable()
  If ActiveDocument.Bookmarks.Exists("mark") Then
  ActiveDocument.Bookmarks("mark").Select
  Set tbl = ActiveDocument.Tables.Add(Range:= _
    Selection.Range, NumRows:=3, NumColumns:=9)
  tbl.AutoFormat Format:=wdTableFormatElegant
  End If
End Sub
```

5 Click the **Run** button to run the macro – see a formatted table appear at the bookmark position

You can use the **Undo** button in Word to reverse the two steps performed by VBA to Add and Format this table.

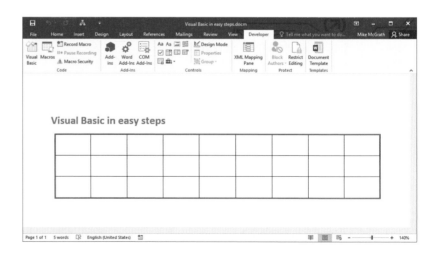

...cont'd

When you have created a macro that you wish to make available for use in other documents, the macro can be stored inside Word's master template **Normal.dotm** and then added as a Word menu item.

1 Select **Developer**, **Macros** to open the **Macros** dialog, then click the **Organizer** button

The **Run** button on the **Macros** dialog can be used to run any macro stored in **Normal.dotm** – without creating a custom menu item.

2 Choose the **Macro Project Items** tab, select the macro module from the current document list, then click the **Copy** button to copy the macro to **Normal.dotm**

3 Close the **Organizer** and the current document, then start a new document and insert a bookmark named "mark"

4 Click **File**, **Options**, **Quick Access Toolbar**, to enter the **Customize the Quick Access Toolbar** dialog

5 In the **Choose Commands from** drop-down, choose **Macros**, then **Add** the **AddTable** module and click **OK** to add an icon to the **Quick Access Toolbar**

6 Click the newly added **AddTable** macro icon on the **Quick Access Toolbar** to run the macro – once more adding the same formatted table at the bookmark position

Creating an Excel macro

Values can be inserted into cells of an Excel spreadsheet by a macro that uses a loop to move through a range of cells.

1 Open a worksheet in Excel then click **Developer**, **Visual Basic**, or press **Alt + F11**, to open the **Visual Basic Editor**

2 In the **Visual Basic Editor**, click **Insert**, **Module** to open the **Code Editor** window

3 Now, type the following code into the **Code Editor**

```
Public Sub AddMonthNames()
Dim i As Integer
i = 0
Do Until i = 12
        Set currentCell = ActiveSheet.Cells( _
          ActiveCell.Row + i , ActiveCell.Column)
        i = i + 1
        currentCell.Font.Bold = True
        currentCell.Font.Color = vbRed
        currentCell.Value = MonthName( i )
Loop
End Sub
```

Hot tip

If the **Developer** tab is not visible, click **File**, **Options**, **Customize Ribbon**, and check the "Developer" box in the **Main Tabs** options.

4 Select any cell in the worksheet then click the **Run** button, to run the macro – you will see bold red month names appear in cells down the current column, starting at the selected cell

Don't forget

VBA has a small range of color constants, like the **vbRed** constant seen here. Refer to VBA Help to discover a full list.

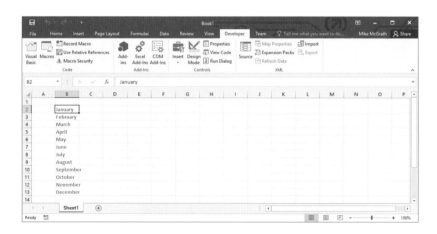

...cont'd

Excel macros can be run automatically when a Worksheet gets
loaded, or manually using a **Button** control.

1 In the Visual Basic
Editor's **Project** window,
right-click on the
ThisWorkbook icon and
choose **View Code** from
the context menu

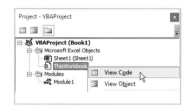

2 From the drop-down list at the top of the **Code Editor**,
select the **Workbook** item then add this code

```
Private Sub Workbook_Open()
MsgBox("Workbook opened at "+ Str(Time) )
End Sub
```

3 On the **Developer** tab, click **Insert**, **ActiveX Controls**
(button) then click an empty cell to add a **Button** control

4 Double-click the **Button** control to open the **Code
Editor** in its **Click** event-handler, then add this statement

```
Call AddMonthNames
```

5 Save the changes and close the
worksheet. Reopen the worksheet
to see the MessageBox appear, then
click the **Button** to run the macro

Use the **Design
Mode** button on the
Developer tab when
you want to edit or
move controls on a
worksheet.

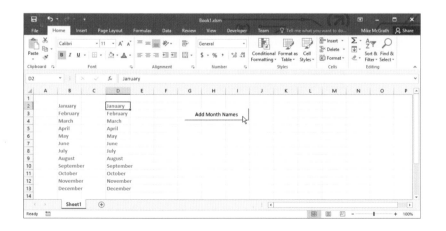

Running advanced macros

More advanced macros can be created to control one Office application from within another. Typically, you may want to include information from an Excel spreadsheet within a Word document, using a macro to get the information automatically.

1 Open Excel and add some data in cell **B2**. Name this cell "Total", save the Workbook as "Sales.xlsx" in your Documents folder, and then close Excel

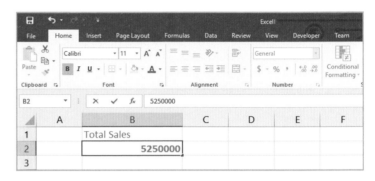

2 Start a new Word document, then insert a **Bookmark** and also name it "Total" – it doesn't need to have the same name as the Excel cell but it is convenient to do so

3 Open the **Visual Basic Editor** then click **Tools**, **References** to launch the **References** dialog – check the **Microsoft Excel Object Library** item, then click **OK**

The version number of the **Microsoft Excel Object Library** will vary according to which Office version you are using.

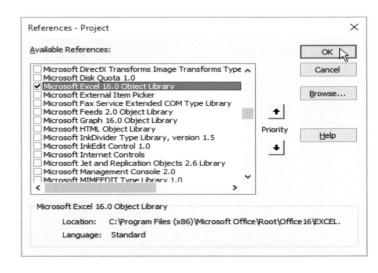

4 In the **Visual Basic Editor,** click **Insert**, **Module** to open the **Code Editor** window

5 Now, type the following code into the **Code Editor**, modifying the path to suit the location of your "Sales.xlsx"

```
Private Sub GetTotal()
Set xl = CreateObject("Excel.Application")
xl.Workbooks.Open ("C:\Users\Mike\Documents\Sales.xlsx")
xl.Worksheets("Sheet1").Activate
ActiveDocument.Bookmarks("Total").Select

Dim sum As String
sum = FormatCurrency( xl.ActiveSheet.Cells( 2, 2 ) )
Selection.InsertAfter (sum)

xl.Workbooks.Close
Set xl = Nothing
End Sub
```

The Excel cell in this example is addressed as **xl.ActiveSheet.Cells(2,2)** – as row 2 and column 2.

6 Click the **Run** button to run the macro, and see the value retrieved from the Excel cell get formatted into the local currency and appear in the Word document

Remember to have the macro close the Workbook and release Excel, after it has retrieved the cell value.

An introduction to VBScript

VBScript is a scripting language that, like VBA, shares the same core Visual Basic language as that found in a Visual Studio IDE. Scripts written in VBScript are interpreted by the **Windows Script Host** VBScript "engine", which processes the instructions to execute the script. The script engine can be invoked either from within the Windows GUI, or at a Windows Command Prompt.

Unlike the Visual Studio IDE and VBA Code Editor in Microsoft Office apps, there is no development environment for VBScript – you simply create your scripts in any plain text editor.

Hello.vbs

1 Open a plain text editor, such as Windows Notepad, then type the following code
MsgBox "Hello from VBScript!", vbExclamation , "Message"

2 Name this file "Hello.vbs" and save it on your Desktop

3 Double-click on the file icon to invoke the **Windows Script Host** VBScript engine from the Windows GUI, to execute the script – you will see the Message Box appear

4 Launch a **Command Prompt** window, then use the CD command to navigate to your Desktop directory

5 Now, type the command "Hello.vbs" and hit **Enter** to invoke the **Windows Script Host** VBScript engine from the Command Prompt – you will see the Message Box appear again

Notice that VBScript does not have any parentheses in the statement that creates the message box dialog.

Enforcing declarations

It is good practice to begin every VBScript with a statement of **Option Explicit**. This is a standard "compiler directive" that must appear at the start of a script, and requires all variables to be explicitly declared with the **Dim** keyword before they can be used. Without this directive, the script can implicitly create variables simply by assigning a value to a variable name of your choice. Although this might seem harmless, it can create unexpected errors that can be difficult to debug. Adding **Option Explicit** at the start of the script provides error-checking to prevent these errors. Its significance can best be understood by a simple example:

1 Create a script that assigns a text string to an implicit variable, to be displayed in a message box dialog
bookTitle = "Visual Basic in easy steps"
MsgBox bookTitle, vbInformation, "Message"

Explicit.vbs

2 Run the script to see that the string fails to appear, as the variable name is misspelled on the second line – the compiler thinks this is just another implicit variable so gives no warning

3 Edit this script by adding these lines, at the very start of the script, to enforce and comply with variable declaration
Option Explicit
Dim bookTitle

4 Run the script once more to see the error clearly identified, as the misspelled variable name has not been declared

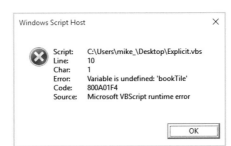

Hot tip

You should always begin each and every VBScript with the **Option Explicit** compiler directive.

5 Correct the spelling error, then run the script to see it now performs as expected

Validating input

VBScript is a topic in itself, but to get a flavor of how it can be used, the rest of this chapter is devoted to three scripts that handle user input, text files, and Windows registry data, respectively.

As with Visual Basic, VBScript can request user data with an input dialog box. The input data is assigned to a variable as a text string that can be examined for validation against requirements, for example, to allow only letters and space characters.

GetName.vbs

1 Start a VBScript with the standard compiler directive, then declare a variable to store input, and a variable to store an expression against which to validate the input
Option Explicit
Dim name, regX

2 Add a function block that assigns input to the **name** variable and has a placeholder for test statements
Private Function GetName()

name = InputBox("What's Your Name?", "Question")

' If-Else statements to be inserted here.

End Function

3 At the placeholder, insert a test to exit the script if the user pushes the "Cancel" button on the input dialog
If VarType(name) = vbEmpty Then
Exit Function

Hot tip

The **VarType()** function returns an integer indicating the data type of the variable. Where the variable is uninitialized (such as when the user presses the Cancel button) it returns zero – equivalent to the constant **vbEmpty**.

4 Next, insert a test to inform the user if they input nothing, then reopen the input dialog so they can try again
Elseif name = "" Then
MsgBox "You didn't input anything", _
vbInformation, "Error"
Call GetName

5 Now, insert a test to inform the user of invalid input, then reopen the input dialog so they can try again
Elseif Invalid() Then
MsgBox "Only A-Z and Spaces Allowed!", _
vbCritical, "Error"
Call GetName

6 Finally, insert a statement to display valid accepted input

```
Else
MsgBox "Welcome " & name & "!" _
            vbExclamation, "Message"
End If
```

7 Add a second function that implements character validation by testing against a Regular Expression

```
Private Function Invalid()
Set regX = New RegExp
regX.Pattern = "[^ A-Z a-z]"
Invalid = regX.Test( Name )
End Function
```

The **RegExp** object has a **Pattern** property that specifies valid characters, and a **Test()** method to compare a specified value against its pattern.

8 At the end of the script, add a statement to call the first function, requesting user input

```
Call GetName
```

9 Run the script and attempt to validate various input

Learn more about Regular Expressions online at **regular-expressions.info**

Merging text files

Just as the previous example made use of a scripting object called "RegExp", which provided special properties and methods to handle Regular Expressions, there is a scripting object called "Scripting.FileSystemObject" that provides special properties and methods to handle a computer's file system.

Once you have created an instance of the **FileSystemObject**, you can open folders and files to read and write within the file system. For example, you can use its methods and properties to copy text from multiple existing files into a single new file.

FileMerge.vbs

1 Create a folder named "Textfiles" on your Desktop, then place several plain text files within that folder

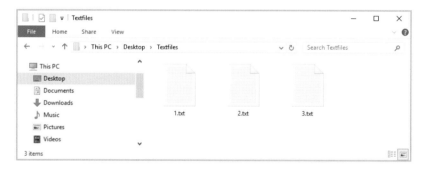

2 Start a VBScript with the standard compiler directive, then declare five variables for text file manipulation
Option Explicit
Dim fso, folder, textOut, file, textIn

Beware

Note that the **GetFolder()** method here specifies the name and path to the folder. If you name your folder differently, or put it elsewhere, you will need to modify those details in the **Set folder** statement.

3 Add a statement to create a **FileSystemObject** instance
Set fso = CreateObject("Scripting.FileSystemObject")

4 Next, add a statement to get a list of the names of all files within the "Textfiles" folder
Set folder = fso.GetFolder(".\Textfiles")

5 Now, add a statement to create a new text file – into which you can copy text from each file within the folder
Set textOut = fso.CreateTextFile("Merged.txt")

6 Add a loop that opens then closes each file within the folder, and has a placeholder for read/write statements
For Each file In folder

    Set textIn = fso.OpenTextFile(file, 1)

    ' Read/write statements to be inserted here.

    textIn.Close

Next

7 At the placeholder, insert statements to write each file's name, text content, and a blank line separator
textOut.WriteLine "File: " & file.Name
textOut.WriteLine textIn.ReadAll
textOut.WriteLine vbCr

8 At the end of the script, after the loop, add a statement to close the new file after all content has been written into it
textOut.Close

9 Save the script on your Desktop, alongside the "Textfiles" folder, then run the script and open the new file it creates

The numeric value specified to the **OpenTextFile()** method indicates the input/ output mode. A value of 1 is ForReading mode, a value of 8 is ForAppending mode.

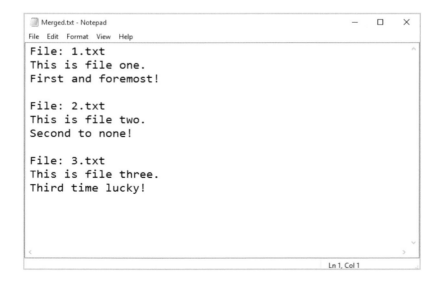

```
File: 1.txt
This is file one.
First and foremost!

File: 2.txt
This is file two.
Second to none!

File: 3.txt
This is file three.
Third time lucky!
```

This script must be in the same directory as the Textfiles folder, or you will need to modify the path in the **Set folder** statement.

Getting registry data

The Windows operating system has a scripting object called "WScript.Shell", which provides special properties and methods to handle environment variables, shortcuts, and Registry components. For example, you can use its methods and properties to get the Windows version name, product ID, and product key. The key is stored in encrypted format, but it can be decrypted by VBScript.

WinInfo.vbs

1 Start a VBScript with the standard compiler directive, then declare five variables for registry manipulation
Option Explicit

Dim wss, dir, sys, pid, bin

2 Add a statement to create a **Shell** object instance
Set wss = CreateObject("WScript.Shell")

3 Next, initialize the remaining four variables with a registry location path and values read from that location
dir = _
"HKLM\SOFTWARE\Microsoft\Windows NT\CurrentVersion\"
sys = "Version: " & _
      wss.RegRead(dir & "ProductName") & vbCr
pid = "ID: " & wss.RegRead(dir & "ProductID") &vbCr
bin = wss.RegRead(dir & "DigitalProductId")

4 Add a statement to display the Windows information
MsgBox sys & pid & "Key: " & Decrypt(bin), _
      vbInformation, "WinInfo"

5 Add a function block that receives the encrypted binary key read from the registry – that is to be decrypted
Private Function Decrypt(bin)

' Statements to be inserted here.

End Function

6 Within the function block, begin by declaring 10 variables, then initialize three of them like this
Dim win, map, i, j, cut, seq, fin, top, add, key

win = (bin(66) \ 6) And 1
bin(66) = (bin(66) And &HF7) Or ((win And 2) * 4)
map = "BCDFGHJKMPQRTVWXY2346789"

Beware

Changing values in the Windows Registry can render your PC useless. This script merely reads existing values without making changes to the Registry.

144

7 Add these nested loops to interpret the encrypted key

```
i = 24
Do
        cut = 0
        j = 14
        Do
                cut = cut * 256
                cut = bin( j + 52 ) + cut
                bin( j + 52 ) = ( cut \ 24 )
                cut = cut Mod 24
                j = j -1
        Loop Until j < 0
        i = i - 1
        seq = Mid( map, cut + 1, 1 ) & seq
        fin = cut
Loop Until i < 0
```

Don't forget

This script example is not intended to be instructional – it merely demonstrates the power of VBScript.

8 Now, add these statements to make substitutions

```
top = Mid( seq, 2, fin )
add = "N"
seq = Replace( seq, top, top & add, 2, 1, 0 )
If fin = 0 Then seq = add & seq
```

9 Add these final statements to format and return the decrypted key to the calling statement for display

```
key = ""
For i = 1 To 25
        key = key + Mid( seq, i, 1 )
        If ( i Mod 5 = 0 ) And ( i < 25 ) Then
                key = key + "-"
        End If
Next
Decrypt = Key
```

Hot tip

From Windows 8 onwards, the product key is no longer visible on a case sticker but is encrypted in the Registry – this script helps you retrieve your key.

10 Run the script to see the Windows version and product information displayed

145

Summary

- Visual Basic for Applications (VBA) is built into all Microsoft Office applications, but each application has unique objects.
- The VBA environment is similar to that of the Visual Studio IDE but it can't produce standalone executable applications.
- A **macro** can insert content into a Word document at the position indicated by an inserted bookmark.
- Saving macros in the **Normal.dotm** master template makes them available for use in other Word documents.
- Loops can be used in a VBA macro to read or write a range of cells within an Excel spreadsheet.
- Advanced macros allow one Office application to be controlled from within another one.
- There is no development environment for VBScript – scripts are created in any plain text editor such as Windows Notepad.
- The script engine that interprets VBScript instructions can be invoked from the Windows GUI or at the Command Prompt.
- Every VBScript should begin with an **Option Explicit** statement to enforce declaration of variables before their use.
- The **VarType()** function that tests variable data types will return a **vbEmpty** zero value when the tested variable is uninitialized.
- A **RegExp** object has a **Pattern** property and a **Test()** method for Regular Expression comparison – such as input validation.
- A **Scripting.FileSystemObject** object has properties and methods to read and write text files on your system.
- The **OpenTextFile()** method must specify whether the file is being opened in ForReading mode or in ForAppending mode.
- A **WScript.Shell** object has properties and methods to handle environment variables, shortcuts, and Registry components.

9 Harnessing data

This chapter shows how Visual Basic applications can import data from a variety of external sources.

Reading text files

The **My.Computer.FileSystem** object has methods that make it easy for Visual Basic applications to work with local files. Text can be imported using its **ReadAllText()** method and exported using its **WriteAllText()** method to append text to an existing file, or to create a new file. Files can be removed with the **DeleteFile()** method or their existence confirmed with the **FileExists()** method.

1 Start a new **Windows Forms Application** then add two **TextBox** controls and three **Button** controls to the Form

2 Set the **Multiline** property of the bottom **TextBox** to **True**, then name the buttons **WriteBtn, ReadBtn, DeleteBtn**

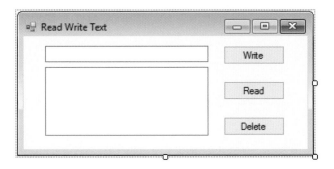

Don't forget

Remember to include the third **True** parameter to append text to a file.

3 Select **View, Code** to open the **Code Editor,** then create a path variable in the declarations section, modifying the path to that of the Documents folder on your system
Dim myFile As String = "C:\Users\Mike\Documents\log.txt"

4 Double-click the **WriteBtn** to open the **Code Editor** and add the following code to its **Click** event-handler

```
My.Computer.FileSystem.WriteAllText( _
        myFile, TextBox1.Text & vbCrLf, True)
TextBox1.Text = ""
```

5 Return to the **Form Designer,** then double-click the **ReadBtn** and add this code to its **Click** event-handler

```
Try
TextBox2.Text = _
My.Computer.FileSystem.ReadAllText( myFile )
Catch ex As Exception
TextBox2.Text = "Unable to read from  " & myFile
End Try
```

6 Return to the **Form Designer**, then double-click the **DeleteBtn** and add this code to its **Click** event-handler
```
TextBox1.Text = ""
TextBox2.Text = ""
If My.Computer.FileSystem.FileExists( myFile ) Then
My.Computer.FileSystem.DeleteFile( myFile )
End If
```

7 Click the **Start** button to run the application, then enter some text into the top **TextBox**

Ensure that the application has permission to write to the log file location.

8 Click the **WriteBtn** to have your text written into a new file and see the top **TextBox** become cleared

9 Click the **ReadBtn** to have the file contents read and see your text appear in the bottom **TextBox**

Remove the log file, then click the **ReadBtn** to attempt to read from the missing file – the **Catch** statement will appear.

10 Repeat steps 7 and 8 to append more lines of text, then click the **DeleteBtn** to remove the file and text content

149

Streaming lines of text

The Visual Basic **System.IO** class can be used to import data and files into an application as a "stream". A stream is more flexible than a file as it can be searched and manipulated. A stream is first created as a new **System.IO.FileStream** object that specifies the file to work with and the operation to perform as its parameters. A new **System.IO.StreamReader** object can then be created to read from an opened file in a variety of ways – its **ReadToEnd()** method will read the entire file. It is important to then release the **StreamReader** and **FileStream** using their **Dispose()** method.

1. Add to a Form an **OpenFileDialog**, a **TextBox** and two **Button** controls named **OpenBtn** and **PrintBtn**

2. Double-click the **OpenBtn Button** to open the **Code Editor**, then add this code to the declarations section
   Dim txt As String

3. Now add the following code to the **OpenBtn Button** control's **Click** event-handler
   ```
   If OpenFileDialog1.ShowDialog = DialogResult.OK Then
   Dim stream As New System.IO.FileStream _
   (OpenFileDialog1.FileName, System.IO.FileMode.Open)
   Dim reader As New System.IO.StreamReader(stream)
   txt = reader.ReadToEnd
   reader.Dispose()
   stream.Dispose()
   TextBox1.Text = txt
   End If
   ```

4. Run the application, then click the **OpenBtn Button** and browse to select a text file for display in the **TextBox**

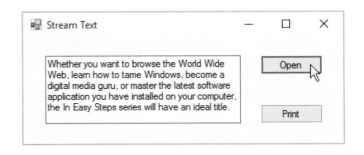

150

...cont'd

Adding Print ability

1 Add both a **PrintDialog** and **PrintDocument** component from the **Printing** section of the **Toolbox**

2 Double-click the **PrintBtn Button** and add the following code to its **Click** event-handler
```
PrintDialog1.AllowSomePages = True
PrintDialog1.ShowHelp = True
If PrintDialog1.ShowDialog = DialogResult.OK Then
        If txt <> "" Then
        PrintDocument1.Print()
        End If
End If
```

This subroutine configures the **Print** dialog, then if the **txt** variable is not empty, calls the **Print()** method of the **PrintDocument1** component. This is not enough to print by itself – it merely fires a **PrintPage** event whose event-handler must be coded to make the application print out the text.

3 Double-click on the **PrintDocument1** icon in the Form Designer's **Component Tray** to open the **Code Editor** in its **PrintPage** event-handler, and type this code
```
e.Graphics.DrawString(txt, Me.Font, Brushes.Black, _
e.MarginBounds, StringFormat.GenericTypographic)
```

In this code the letter "e" is specified in the event-handler's parameters to represent a **PrintPageEventArgs** object, that uses the **Graphics.DrawString()** method to print the text.

4 Click the **Start** button to run the application and use the **OpenBtn Button** to choose a text file, then click the **PrintBtn Button** to send it to your printer

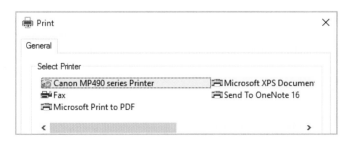

The **PrintDialog** component lets your application launch the Windows **Print** dialog – but you need to add a **PrintDocument** component to actually print anything.

151

Further code would need to be added to the **PrintPage** event-handler to allow the printer to handle multiple pages.

Reading Excel spreadsheets

Data contained within an Excel spreadsheet can be imported into an application, where the value of each cell can be conveniently stored in a two-dimensional array, representing rows and columns. This allows each individual cell to be addressed using the same row and column number that it has in the spreadsheet – for instance, **cell(2,3)** could address the third cell on the second row.

1 Create an Excel Workbook called "Data.xlsx" with the data values below, and save it in your **Documents** folder

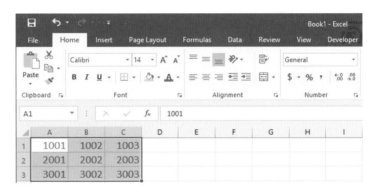

2 Start a new **Windows Forms Application**, then add three **ListBox** and **Label** controls, and a **Button** to the Form

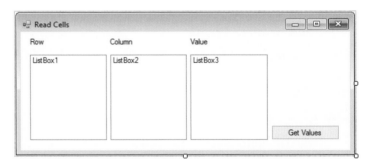

Refer to page 136 for an illustration of the **References** dialog – compare the similarities in this example with the VBA example listed there.

3 Click **Project**, **Add Reference** to launch the **Add Reference** dialog, then choose the **Microsoft Excel Object Library** item on the **COM** tab and click **OK**

4 Select View, Code to open the Code Editor, then create a path variable to the spreadsheet in the declarations section
Dim mySS As String = "C:\Users\Mike\Documents\Data.xlsx"

...cont'd

5 Double-click the **Button** control to open the **Code Editor**, and type this code into its **Click** event-handler

```
Dim row, col, finalRow, finalCol As Integer
Dim xl = CreateObject("Excel.Application")
xl.Workbooks.Open( mySS )
xl.Worksheets("Sheet1").Activate()
finalRow = xl.ActiveSheet.UsedRange.Rows.Count
finalCol = xl.ActiveSheet.UsedRange.Columns.Count
Dim vals(finalRow, finalCol) As String
```

This opens the worksheet, counts the number of used rows and columns, then creates a two-dimensional array of the same size.

6 Add this loop to assign the cell values to the array elements and to display them in the **ListBox** controls

```
For row = 1 To finalRow
        For col = 1 To finalCol
        vals(row, col) = _
                Str(xl.ActiveSheet.Cells(row, col).Value)
        ListBox1.Items.Add(row)
        ListBox2.Items.Add(col)
        ListBox3.Items.Add( vals(row, col) )
        Next col
Next row
```

7 Finally, add these two lines to release the resources, then run the application and click the **Button**

```
xl.Workbooks.Close()
xl = Nothing
```

Many examples in this book benefit by enclosure in a **Try Catch** statement, but they are not listed in order to save space – add one to this example to catch the exception that would be thrown if the worksheet could not be read.

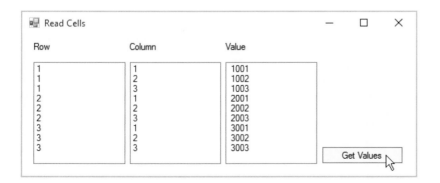

See page 63 for more on multi-dimensional arrays.

Reading XML files

The Visual Basic **System.Xml** object can be used to easily import data into an application from an XML document. A container for the data is first created as a **System.Xml.XmlDocument** object, then the data is loaded into it using its **Load()** method to copy data from the XML document file.

A **System.Xml.XmlNodeList** can then create an **Item()** array of all the elements in the XML document. Individual elements can be addressed by stating their name as the parameter to the **SelectSingleNode()** method of the **Item()** array, and the value contained within that element retrieved by its **InnerText** property.

 1 Open any plain text editor, such as **Notepad**, and create an XML document with elements like those below – name it **books.xml** and save it in the **Documents** folder

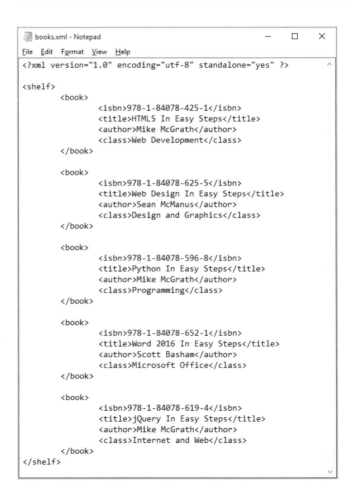

You can download the XML document shown here, along with all the other files used in this book, from **www.ineasysteps.com/resource-centre/downloads/**

2 Start a new **Windows Forms Application** and add a **ListBox** and a **Button** to the Form

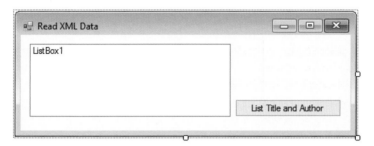

3 Double-click the **Button** to open the **Code Editor** and type this code into its **Click** event-handler, to create an **XmlDocument** object from the XML file

```
Dim doc As New System.Xml.XmlDocument
doc.Load( "C:\Users\Mike\Documents\books.xml" )
```

4 Add the following code to create an **XmlNodeList** from the **<book>** elements and their nested elements

```
Dim nodes As System.Xml.XmlNodeList
nodes = doc.SelectNodes( "shelf/book" )
```

5 Now, add a loop to display the text contained in each **<title>** and **<author>** element, then run the application

```
Dim counter = 0
Do Until counter = nodes.Count
ListBox1.Items.Add(nodes.Item(counter) _
  .SelectSingleNode("title").InnerText & " by " _
& nodes.Item(counter) _
  .SelectSingleNode("author").InnerText & vbCrLf)
counter += 1
Loop
```

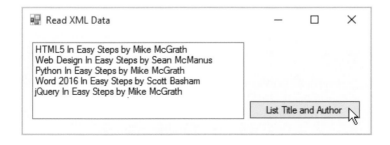

Notice how the **Count** property of the **XmlNodeList** is used to set the limit of the loop.

Creating an XML dataset

Visual Basic provides specialized components for working with data in table format, such as that contained in XML elements or database tables. These components can be found in the **Toolbox**, under the **Data** heading.

The **DataSet** component can be added to an application, to create a table in the system memory that can be loaded with data from any suitable source. Most often it is convenient to display the table data in the interface using a **DataGridView** component. This allows the data stored in memory to be dynamically manipulated within the application, then written back to a file.

1 Start a new **Windows Forms Application** and add a **DataGridView** component and two **Button** controls to the Form – name the buttons **ReadBtn** and **WriteBtn**

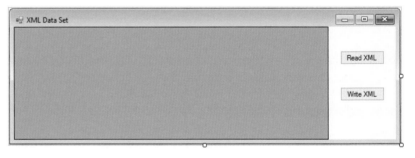

2 Double-click the **DataSet** item in the **Toolbox**, then choose the **Untyped DataSet** option in the **Add DataSet** dialog, and click **OK** – see the **DataSet** icon appear on the **Component Tray** in the Form Designer

Here, the document file **books.xml** must be located in the **Documents** directory – adjust the path to suit your system.

3 Double-click the **ReadBtn Button** to open the **Code Editor**, then type this code into its **Click** event-handler to create a **DataSet** from the XML document on page 154
```
DataSet1.ReadXml( "C:\Users\Mike\Documents\books.xml" )
```

4 Add this code to load those elements nested under the **<book>** element from the **DataSet** into the **DataGridView** control
```
DataGridView1.DataSource = DataSet1
DataGridView1.DataMember = "book"
```

...cont'd

5 Return to the **Form Designer** then double-click the **WriteBtn Button** and add this code to its event-handler
DataSet1.WriteXml("C:\Users\Mike\Documents\books.xml")

6 Click the **Start** button to run the application, then click the **ReadBtn Button** to load the **DataSet** data into the **DataGridView** control

	isbn	title	author	class
▶	978-1-84078-425-1	HTML5 In Easy Steps	Mike McGrath	Web Development
	978-1-84078-625-5	Web Design In Easy Steps	Sean McManus	Design and Graphics
	978-1-84078-596-8	Python In Easy Steps	Mike McGrath	Programming
	978-1-84078-652-1	Word 2016 In Easy Steps	Scott Basham	Microsoft Office
	978-1-84078-619-4	jQuery In Easy Steps	Mike McGrath	Internet and Web

XML Data Set — Read XML / Write XML buttons

Hot tip
You can set a DataGridView's **AutoSizeColumnsMode** property to **AllCells**, to automatically show all text content in each cell.

The **DataGridView** control displays the element name as the heading for each column and the element content on each row of that column. Initially, the first cell on the first row is in focus, but you can click on any other cell to move the focus. When you double-click the cell in focus it changes into edit mode where you can update its content.

7 Add another row of data to the last row of the table, then click the **WriteBtn** control to save the amended data

	isbn	title	author	class
	978-1-84078-425-1	HTML5 In Easy Steps	Mike McGrath	Web Development
	978-1-84078-625-5	Web Design In Easy Steps	Sean McManus	Design and Graphics
	978-1-84078-596-8	Python In Easy Steps	Mike McGrath	Programming
	978-1-84078-652-1	Word 2016 In Easy Steps	Scott Basham	Microsoft Office
	978-1-84078-619-4	jQuery In Easy Steps	Mike McGrath	Internet and Web
▶	978-1-84078-643-9	Windows 10 In Easy Steps	Nick Vandome	Operating Systems

XML Data Set — Read XML / Write XML buttons

Beware
ScrollBars will, by default, automatically appear when the cell content overflows the DataGridView control. Setting its **ScrollBars** property to **None** can hide content from view.

8 Restart the application, then click the **ReadBtn Button** to once more load the XML data into the **DataGridView** control – see that the row you added has been preserved

157

Reading RSS feeds

Live XML data can be imported from outside the local system into a Visual Basic application using a **Rich Site Summary/Really Simple Syndication (RSS)** feed. This delivers the XML data as a stream that can be stored within a **System.Xml.XmlDocument** object, like that used to store data from an XML file on page 155.

1 Start a new **Windows Forms Application**, then add a **GroupBox, Label, Button,** and **TextBox** control to the Form

2 Name the **TextBox** as "ZipCode" and set its **Text** property to "10021" – a New York City Zip code. Arrange the controls so your Form looks like this:

You can find the **GroupBox** control in the **Containers** section of the **Toolbox**.

3 To create a request to the **Yahoo! Weather RSS Feed** for the Zip code above, double-click the **Button** and type the following code into its **Click** event-handler
```
Dim rssUrl = _
        "http://xml.weather.yahoo.com/forecastrss?p=" _
        + ZipCode.Text
Dim rssRequest As System.Net.WebRequest = _
        System.Net.WebRequest.Create(rssUrl)
```

This example relies upon the format of an external XML document – if the format gets changed, it may need amending to run correctly. You can discover the latest details about the Yahoo! Weather RSS Feed online at **developer.yahoo.com/weather/**

4 Save the response data into a **Stream** object by adding these two statements
```
Dim rssResponse As System.Net.WebResponse = _
        rssRequest.GetResponse()
Dim rssStream As System.IO.Stream = _
        rssReponse.GetResponseStream
```

158

...cont'd

5 Type the code below to load the saved data stream into an **XmlDocument** object

```
Dim rssDoc As New System.Xml.XmlDocument
rssDoc.Load(rssStream)
```

6 Create an **XmlNodeList** under the **<channel>** element of the **XmlDocument** object by adding these lines:

```
Dim nodes As System.Xml.XmlNodeList
nodes = rssDoc.SelectNodes("/rss/channel")
```

You need an internet connection to run this application successfully.

7 Now, add this code to display the content contained in the **<title>** element of the **XmlDocument** object

```
GroupBox1.Text = _
nodes.Item(0).SelectSingleNode("title").InnerText
```

8 Run the application and click the **OK** button to test the RSS request – after a short delay, see the **GroupBox Text** property change to the title of the response document

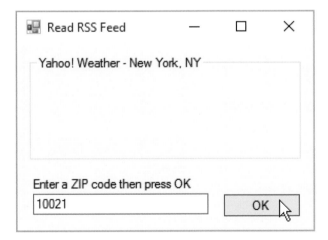

Change the value in the **TextBox** to any other valid US Zip code, then click **OK** to see the title change again – for instance, try 90021.

When the application is able to retrieve the title from the XML response document, you can proceed to add further code, as described on the next page, to extract information from the document about the current weather conditions.

Addressing XML attributes

The XML response document sent from Yahoo! Weather, in response to the RSS request made by the application on the previous page, contains information about the current weather conditions for the specified Zip code.

The details are assigned to attributes of XML elements that each have a **yweather:** namespace prefix. To access XML namespace elements in Visual Basic it is necessary to first create an **XmlNamespaceManager** object, then specify the namespace name and URL as parameters to its **AddNamespace()** method. Once an **XmlNamespaceManager** has been created, you simply add its name as a second parameter to each **SelectSingleNode()** call.

① Add three **TextBox** controls and three **Label** controls to the Form in the previous example

② Name the **TextBox** controls **Climate**, **Temperature**, and **Humidity**, then set the **Text** property of each **Label** control accordingly

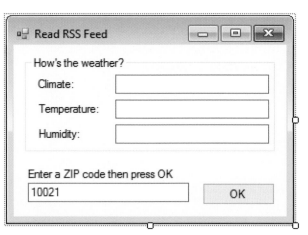

Information, such as the namespace URL, are given in the instructions provided by Yahoo! on how to use their RSS Weather feed.

③ Double-click the **OK** Button to open the **Code Editor** and append the following code after the earlier code in its **Click** event-handler – to create a new instance of the **XmlNamespaceManager** object

```
Dim nsMgr = New _
System.Xml.XmlNamespaceManager(rssDoc.NameTable)
nsMgr.AddNamespace("yweather", _
        "http://xml.weather.yahoo.com/ns/rss/1.0")
```

4 Add this code to display the current weather condition

```
Climate.Text = rssDoc.SelectSingleNode( _
"/rss/channel/item/yweather:condition/@text", _
        nsMgr).InnerText
```

5 Add this code to display the current temperature

```
Temperature.Text = rssDoc.SelectSingleNode( _
"/rss/channel/yweather:wind/@chill", _
        nsMgr).InnerText + " F"
```

6 Add this code to display the current humidity

```
Humidity.Text = rssDoc.SelectSingleNode( _
"/rss/channel/yweather:atmosphere/@humidity", _
        nsMgr).InnerText + " %"
```

7 Surround the entire code inside the **Click** event-handler with a **Try Catch** statement – to catch the exception that will be thrown in the event that the RSS feed is not accessible

8 Run the application, then click the **OK** button to retrieve the current weather information for the specified Zip code from the RSS feed

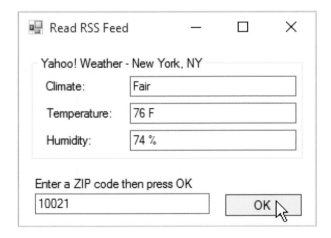

Notice how the @ character is used here in the URL to denote the name of an attribute.

You can see more about **Try Catch** statements back on pages 106-107.

Summary

- The **My.Computer.FileSystem** object can be used to read and write files on your computer.

- A **System.IO.Stream** object can store text that has been read from a local file or external source, such as a web response.

- It is important to dispose of **System.IO.Stream** and **System.IO.StreamReader** objects after they have been used.

- The **Print()** method of a **PrintDocument** component does not actually send data to your printer – it only fires a **PrintPage** event whose event-handler must be coded in order to print.

- Data imported from an Excel spreadsheet can best be stored in a two-dimensional array, representing rows and columns.

- The **System.Xml.XmlDocument** object is used to store a representation of an XML document.

- A **System.Xml.XmlNodeList** object creates an **Item()** array of elements selected from a **System.Xml.XmlDocument**.

- The **InnerText** property of a node contains the actual content of that element.

- A **DataSet** component creates a table in system memory that can be loaded with data from any suitable source.

- It is often convenient to display **DataSet** table data in a **DataGridView** component – where it can be modified then written from system memory back to the original source.

- An application can request an RSS feed using a **System.Net.WebRequest** object.

- A **System.Net.WebResponse** object handles the response received after requesting an RSS feed.

- XML elements that have a namespace prefix can be addressed after creating a **System.Xml.NamespaceManager** object.

10 Employing databases

This chapter introduces databases, and demonstrates how to add powerful database functionality to a Visual Basic application with SQL Server.

An introduction to databases

Databases are simply convenient storage containers that store data in a structured manner. Every database is composed of one or more tables that structure the data into organized rows and columns. This makes it easy to reference and manipulate the data. Each database table column has a label to identify the data stored within the table cells in that column. Each row is an entry called a "record" that places data in each cell along that row, like this:

MemberID	Forename	Surname
1	John	Smith
2	Ann	Jones
3	Mike	McGrath

The rows of a database table are not automatically arranged in any particular order, so they can be sorted alphabetically, numerically, or by any other criteria. It is important, therefore, to have some means to identify each record in the table. The example above allocates a "MemberID" for this purpose, and this unique identifier is known as the **Primary Key** for that table.

Storing data in a single table is useful, but relational databases with multiple tables introduce more possibilities by allowing the stored data to be combined in a variety of ways. For example, the table below could be added to the database containing the table shown above.

Beware

Spaces are not allowed in label names – so you should use "MemberID" instead of "Member ID".

VideoID	Title	MemberID
1	Titanic	2
2	Fantasia	3
3	Star Wars	1

The table lists video titles sorted numerically by "VideoID", and describes a relationship linking each member to their hired video:
John (**MemberID #1**) has Star Wars (**VideoID #3**)
Ann (**MemberID #2**) has Titanic (**VideoID #1**)
Mike (**MemberID #3**) has Fantasia (**VideoID #2**).

In this table, the **VideoID** column has the **Primary Key** values identifying title records, and the **MemberID** column contains **Foreign Key** values that reference member name records in the first table.

SQL Server

The SQL Server DataBase Management System (DBMS) that can be bundled with Visual Studio adheres to the relational model like other Relational DataBase Management System (RDBMS) software, such as Oracle or IBM DB2. This means that it observes "normalization" rules that you need to be aware of when designing a database.

Data normalization

Normalization rules insist that data is organized efficiently, and without duplication or redundancy, in order to reduce the potential for anomalies when performing data operations. They require each table to have a **Primary Key** column, and permissible data types must be defined for all other columns. This determines whether cells in the column may contain text or numbers, within a specified range, and whether cells may be left empty or not. In considering the design of a database, normalization sensibly requires data to appear only once – so any repeated data should be moved into its own table then referenced where required. For example, where customer name and address details are repeated in two tables, they should be moved to their own table which can then be referenced from each of the two original tables. This makes it easier to update the customer details without the possibility of creating an anomaly by updating just one set of data.

Data integrity

Another important aspect of RDBMS software concerns the preservation of data integrity by prohibiting "orphaned" records. This means that records that are referenced in another table cannot be deleted unless the reference is first deleted. Otherwise, the reference would become orphaned as it could not find the data in its "parent" table. For example, where a table of customer order details contains a reference to a record in a table of products, the RDBMS software will not allow the product record to be deleted, as doing so would render the customer order reference useless.

A **Foreign Key** always references a **Primary Key** in another table – name them both alike for easy recognition.

The SQL Server Data Tools should have been installed along with Visual Basic – see the installation components on page 11. If they weren't, run the installer, click **Modify**, then check **Microsoft SQL Server Data Tools** and install them.

Designing a database

The process of database design is typically one of refinement to recognize the rules of normalization. Start out with a single table design for all data fields then move those which are repeating into their own table.

Consider the design for a database to store data about an imaginary range of motorcycles, comprising "Sport", "Cruiser", and "Touring" models that are selectively available in "Standard", "Deluxe" and "Classic" versions, and where each model/version has a unique price. A single **Bikes** table of the entire range, plus a column for individual notes, might look like this:

BikeID	Model	Version	Price	Note
1	Sport	Standard	5000	
2	Sport	Deluxe	5500	
3	Cruiser	Standard	6000	
4	Cruiser	Deluxe	6500	
5	Cruiser	Classic	7000	
6	Touring	Standard	8000	
7	Touring	Classic	9000	

The **BikeID** column provides a unique identifier for each row and can be set as the **Primary Key** for the table. The **Price** column contains unique values, and all cells in the **Note** column are initially empty. **Model** and **Version** columns both contain repeated data in contravention of the normalization rules, so they should each be moved into separate tables like those below:

A **Primary Key** uniquely identifies a row within a database table – so a Primary Key value should never be changed.

ModelID	Model
1	Sport
2	Cruiser
3	Touring

VersionID	Version
1	Standard
2	Deluxe
3	Classic

166

The **ModelID** and **VersionID** columns provide a unique identifier for each row and can be set as the **Primary Key** (PK) for their table. They can also be used as a **Foreign Key** (FK) in the refined **Bikes** table below:

BikeID (PK)	ModelID (FK)	VersionID (FK)	Price	Note
1	1	1	5000	
2	1	2	5500	
3	2	1	6000	
4	2	2	6500	
5	2	3	7000	
6	3	1	8000	
7	3	3	9000	

In considering permissible data types for each column, in line with normalization rules, the **BikeID**, **ModelID**, **VersionID**, and **Price** columns should each allow only integer values. The **Model** and **Version** columns should only allow up to 10 characters, and the **Note** column should allow up to, say, 50 various characters. All except the **Note** column are required to contain data – in database terms they should be "Not Null". The database diagram below illustrates these data constraints and the table relationships:

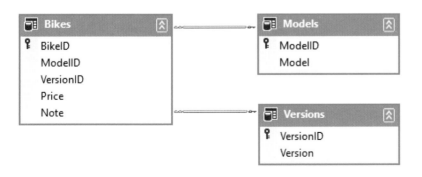

In setting data constraints, consider future eventualities – might a new **Model** or **Version** perhaps have a name longer than 10 characters?

This design is used on the ensuing pages to create an SQL Server database and a Visual Basic application that can communicate with it to dynamically retrieve and manipulate data.

Creating a database

SQL Server is well integrated with Visual Studio so you can easily create a new database from within the IDE.

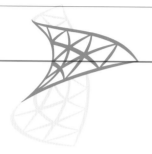

1 Start a new **Windows Forms Application** project and name it "BikesApplication"

2 Click **View**, **Solution Explorer** – to open the Solution Explorer window

3 In the **Solution Explorer** window, right-click on the **VB BikesApplication** icon, then choose **Add**, **New Item** from the menu – to launch the **Add New Item** dialog

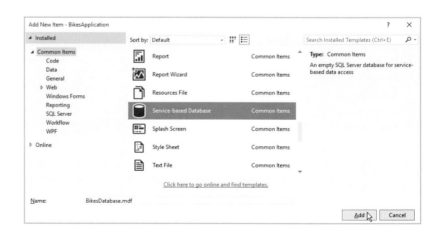

4 In the **Add New Item** dialog, select the **Service-based Database** icon, type "BikesDatabase.mdf" in the name field, then click the **Add** button

If the **Service-based Database** fails to be added, you may need to install SQL Server Data Tools. Run the Visual Studio Community installer, click **Modify** and select **Microsoft SQL Server Data Tools**, install them, and then restart your PC.

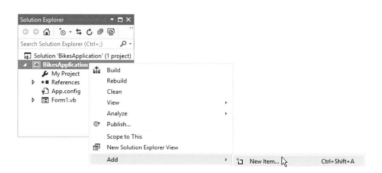

Connecting to a database

1 In **Solution Explorer**, right-click the **BikesDatabase.mdf** icon that has been added, then choose **Open** from the context menu – to open the **Server Explorer** window

2 Examine the **BikesDatabase.mdf** icon in **Server Explorer** and you should see it has an "electric-plug" icon below it to indicate you are connected to that database

3 Right-click the **BikesDatabase.mdf** icon in **Server Explorer** then choose **Close Connection** on the context menu – see the icon change to indicate no connection

4 Next, right-click the **BikesDatabase.mdf** icon in **Server Explorer**, then choose **Refresh** to reconnect to the database

– see that the icon has the "electric-plug" below it once more, indicating you are connected again

5 Now, right-click the **BikesDatabase.mdf** icon again and choose **Modify Connection**, to launch the **Modify Connection** dialog, and click its **Test Connection** button

6 See the **Test connection succeeded** confirmation dialog appear, then click the **OK** button on both dialogs to close them

Hot tip

You can open the **Server Explorer** window by choosing **View**, **Server Explorer** on the menu bar, or with a double-click on the **BikesDatabase.mdf** icon in **Solution Explorer**.

Beware

This chapter builds a complete database application. To recreate this application it is important you carefully follow each step, in precisely the same sequence, in order to avoid errors later.

Adding database tables

Having created the **BikesDatabase** database on the previous page, you can begin to add the **Bikes**, **Models**, and **Versions** tables from the database design on page 167 by creating the tables and setting the **Primary Key** column for each table.

When working with table **Design**, you can close the **Form Designer** window to clean up the IDE.

1 In **Server Explorer**, right-click on the **Tables** icon and choose **Add New Table** from the context menu – to open the **Table Designer** window

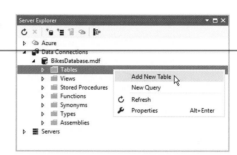

2 In **Table Designer**, type "BikeID" in the field below the **Name** heading – this will be the table's **Primary Key**

3 Click below the **Data Type** heading, then choose the **int** item from the drop-down options – to allow only integer data values for the **BikeID**

4 Ensure that the **Allow Nulls** checkbox is not checked – so empty cells will not be allowed in this column

The table should have a key icon in the box before the name, denoting this as the primary key. If it doesn't, right-click in that box and choose **Set Primary Key**.

5 Right-click on the **BikeID** box and choose **Properties** – to open that column's properties dialog

6 In **Properties**, expand the **Identity Specification** item, then set its **Is Identity** property to **True** – to have the column automatically number its rows

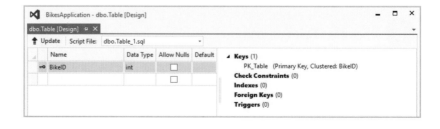

7 By default, a new table is named "Table". Edit this name in the **T-SQL** (Transact SQL) code area at the bottom of the **Table Designer** to rename this table "Bikes"

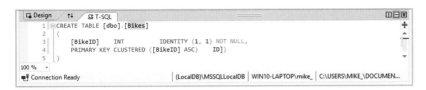

You can double-click any table icon in **Server Explorer** to reopen that table in **Table Designer**.

8 Click the **Update** link at the top left of the table **Design** window, to open the **Preview Database Updates** dialog, then click the **Update Database** button to create the table

9 Precisely repeat each of these steps to create the **Models** table, with a "ModelID" **Primary Key**, and to create the **Versions** table with a "VersionID" **Primary Key**

10 In **Server Explorer**, right-click the **Tables** icon and choose **Refresh** to see your updates applied here – icons appear for all the new tables you have created

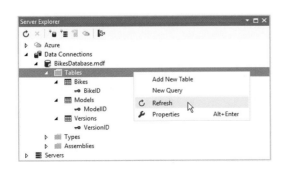

See the table names also change in the **Table Designer** when you apply your updates.

Defining table columns

Having created the **Bikes**, **Models**, and **Versions** tables on the previous page, you can begin to define other columns for each table, setting their **Name**, **Data Type**, and **Allow Nulls**.

1 In **Server Explorer**, right-click on the **Bikes** table icon in the **Tables** folder, then choose **Open Table Definition** from the context menu to open it in **Table Designer**

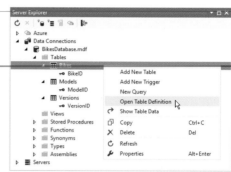

2 Click the next line under the **Name** heading, below the box containing the **BikeID** name, then type "ModelID" to name that column, set the data type to **int** and uncheck the **Allow Nulls** checkbox

3 Repeat step 2 to define the **VersionID** and **Price** columns

4 Add a column named **Note**, set the data type to **varchar(50)** and <u>do</u> check the **Allow Nulls** checkbox – so the completed table definition looks like this:

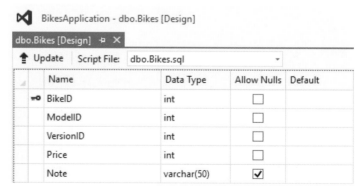

	Name	Data Type	Allow Nulls	Default
🔑	BikeID	int	☐	
	ModelID	int	☐	
	VersionID	int	☐	
	Price	int	☐	
	Note	varchar(50)	☑	

5 In **Server Explorer**, double-click on the **Models** table icon, or choose **Open Table Definition** from the right-click context menu, to open it in **Table Designer**

The **Note** column is the only column in any of these tables that is permitted to contain an empty cell.

6 Click the next line under the **Name** heading, below the box containing the **ModelID** name, then type "Model" to name that column, set the data type to **char(10)** and uncheck the **Allow Nulls** checkbox

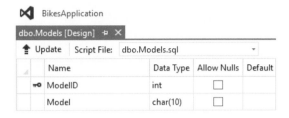

When a table is open in **Table Designer** you can click **View**, **Properties Window** to discover properties of that table.

7 In **Server Explorer**, double-click on the **Versions** table icon to open it in **Table Designer**

8 Click the next line under the **Name** heading, below the box containing the **VersionID** name, then type "Version" to name that column, set the data type to **char(10)** and uncheck the **Allow Nulls** checkbox

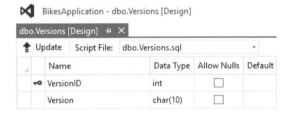

9 Apply all the table updates, then **Refresh** the database contents in **Server Explorer**

10 Expand the tables in **Server Explorer** – to see all the defined columns you have created

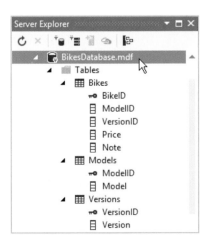

Making table relationships

Having defined all the table columns on the previous page, you can now establish the relationship between the tables to recognize the links for the **Bikes** table's **ModelID** column to the **Models** table, and its **VersionID** column to the **Versions** table.

1 In **Server Explorer**, right-click on the **Bikes** table icon then choose **Open Table Definition** from the menu

2 Right-click on the **Foreign Keys** item in the right pane, then choose **Add New Foreign Key** from the menu

You can use the **Switch to T-SQL Pane** option to open the code area full-screen, then tab between **Table Designer** and the **T-SQL** code window.

```
◢ Keys (1)
      <unnamed>   (Primary Key, Clustered: BikeID)
   Check Constraints (0)
   Indexes (0)
   Foreign Keys (0)
   Triggers (0)        Add New Foreign Key
                       Switch to T-SQL Pane
```

3 Click anywhere on the pane and see a line get added to the **T-SQL** code area at the bottom of **Table Designer** – this must be edited to describe the table relationship

```
CONSTRAINT [FK_Bikes_ToTable] FOREIGN KEY ([Column]) REFERENCES [ToTable]([ToTableColumn])
```

4 Rename the **CONSTRAINT** from "FK_Bikes_ToTable" to **FK_Bikes_To_Models**

5 Rename the **FOREIGN KEY** from "Column" to **ModelID**

6 Rename the **REFERENCES** from "ToTable (ToTableColumn)" to **Models (ModelID)**

The **Constraint** name simply describes the names of the two tables associated by the **Foreign Key**.

```
CONSTRAINT [FK_Bikes_To_Models] FOREIGN KEY ([ModelID]) REFERENCES [Models]([ModelID])
```

7 Click the **Update** link at the top left of the **Table Designer** window, then click the **Update Database** button to create the **Foreign Key** associating the **Bikes** and **Models** tables

8 Right-click on the **Foreign Keys** item in the right pane, then again choose **Add New Foreign Key** from the menu

9 Click anywhere on the pane and once more see a line get added to the **T-SQL** code area in **Table Designer**

```
CONSTRAINT [FK_Bikes_ToTable] FOREIGN KEY ([Column]) REFERENCES [ToTable]([ToTableColumn])
```

10 Rename the **CONSTRAINT** from "FK_Bikes_ToTable" to **FK_Bikes_To_Versions**

11 Rename the **FOREIGN KEY** from "Column" to **VersionID**

12 Rename the **REFERENCES** from "ToTable (ToTableColumn)" to **Versions (VersionID)**

```
CONSTRAINT [FK_Bikes_To_Versions] FOREIGN KEY ([VersionID]) REFERENCES [Versions]([VersionID])
```

13 Click the **Update** link at the top left of the **Table Designer** window, then click the **Update Database** button to create the **Foreign Key** associating the **Bikes** and **Versions** tables

14 The new **Foreign Key** items now appear listed in the right pane in **Table Designer**

```
▲ Keys (1)
      <unnamed>  (Primary Key, Clustered: BikeID)
  Check Constraints (0)
  Indexes (0)
▲ Foreign Keys (2)
      FK_Bikes_To_Models  (ModelID)
      FK_Bikes_To_Versions  (VersionID)
  Triggers (0)
```

The **Foreign Keys** are associating the **ModelID** and **VersionID** columns in the **Bikes** table with the **Primary Keys** in the **Models** and **Versions** tables.

Entering table data

Having established the tables relationship on the previous page, you can now begin to enter actual data records into each table.

1 In **Server Explorer**, expand the **Tables** tree then right-click on the **Models** table icon and choose **Show Table Data** from the menu, to open that table in the **Table Data** window

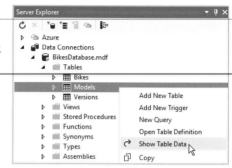

2 Click under the **Model** heading and type "Sport", then press **Tab** twice to move to the **Model** column on the next row – see numbering automatically appear in the **ModelID** column as its **Is Identity** property is set to **True**

3 Type "Cruiser" on the second row and "Touring" on the third row, so the table looks like this – then click the **X** button to close this window

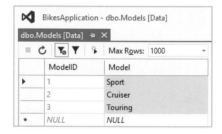

4 Open the **Versions** table in the **Table Data** window, then under the **Version** column, enter "Standard" on the first row, "Deluxe" on the second and "Classic" on the third row – then click the **X** button to close this window

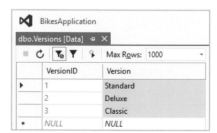

Hot tip

You can move from row to row and from column to column using the arrow keys on your keyboard.

...cont'd

5 Open the **Bikes** table in the **Table Data** window, then enter the data from the table on page 167 – use the **Tab** key to move through the cells to enter **ModelID**, **VersionID**, and **Price** data so the table looks like this:

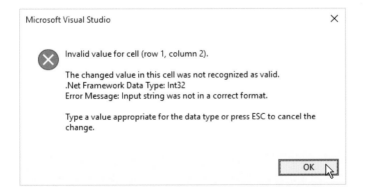

If you encounter an error message when entering table data, it is probably because the table constraints do not allow that entry – check the table definition to correct the problem.

6 To test that the table constraints are working correctly, click the **ModelID** cell on row 1 and change its value to text, then press the **Tab** key – an error dialog should appear complaining that this entry is invalid

Microsoft Visual Studio

Invalid value for cell (row 1, column 2).

The changed value in this cell was not recognized as valid.
.Net Framework Data Type: Int32
Error Message: Input string was not in a correct format.

Type a value appropriate for the data type or press ESC to cancel the change.

OK

You can test the **Foreign Key** constraints are working by trying to delete any row from the **Models** or **Versions** table – you should see a dialog appear saying you cannot do so.

7 Press the **Esc** key to revert back to the original cell value, then click the **X** button to close the **Table Data** window

Creating a database dataset

Having created a database with related tables and data entries over the last few pages, you can now proceed to develop the **BikesApplication** program to incorporate the data as a **Dataset**.

1 Click **View**, **Other Windows**, **Data Sources** on the menu bar – to open the **Data Sources** window

2 In the **Data Sources** window, click **Add New Data Source** – to open the **Data Source Configuration Wizard**

3 Select the **Database** icon and click **Next** to proceed, then select the **Dataset** icon and click **Next** once more

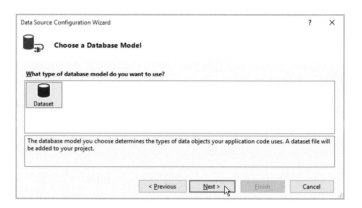

Hot tip

You can click the + button to view the Connection string.

4 Select **BikesDatabase.mdf** as the chosen connection in the drop-down list, then click **Next** to continue

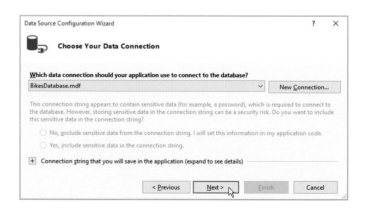

5 Check the **Yes, save the connection as:** checkbox, to save the "BikesDatabaseConnectionString", then click **Next**

6 Check the **Tables** checkbox, to include all the database tables in the dataset, then click the **Finish** button

7 In **Solution Explorer**, you will see that the **Dataset** has been created as a new XML Schema Document (**.xsd**) and the application configuration is stored in an XML document named **App.config**

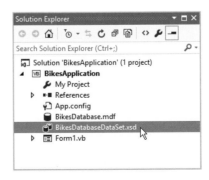

A **Dataset** is an in-memory representation of the tables in the database which can be manipulated before writing data back to the tables.

Adding form data controls

Having created a database **Dataset** on the previous page, you are now ready to add controls to the Form to display the data.

The arrow button will not appear in the **Data Sources** window unless **Form Designer** is open.

1 In **Solution Explorer**, double-click on the **Form1.vb** icon to open the empty form in **Form Designer**

2 Click **View**, **Other Windows**, **Data Sources** to open the **Data Sources** window

3 Select the **Bikes** icon, then click on the dropdown arrow button that appears and choose the **Details** option

4 Expand the **Bikes** tree, select any item then click the arrow button that appears to see a list of possible controls. Choose **ComboBox** for **ModelID** and **VersionID** columns, and choose **TextBox** for all other columns

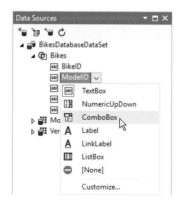

The icon against each item in the **Bikes** list indicates the type of control it will appear in.

5 Get ready to experience one of the most stunning features in Visual Studio! Click on the **Bikes** icon in the **Data Sources** window, then drag it across the IDE and drop it onto the empty form in **Form Designer** – see lots of controls get automatically added to the Form and see these five items get added to the **Component Tray**

Two **ComboBox** and three **Textbox** controls are added to the Form, as specified in the **Data Sources** drop-down list, plus a navigation **ToolStrip** and **Label** controls matching the column headings.

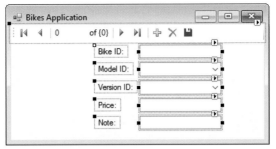

The items added to the **Component Tray** are non-visual components to manage the data flow:

● **TableAdapterManager** is the top-level component that co-ordinates the update operations of **TableAdapters**.

● **TableAdapter** is the data access object that has **Fill()** and **GetData()** methods to actually supply data to the controls.

● **DataSet** contains data tables of the in-memory representation of the database tables.

● **BindingSource** is an intermediate manager between the dataset and Form controls.

● **BindingNavigator** supports the navigation **ToolStrip** to move through the records, and allows data to be added or deleted.

⑥ Press the **Start** button to run the application and try out the navigation controls – you will see the **Bikes** table data appear in the **TextBox** and **ComboBox** controls

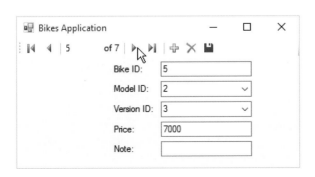

You can view a graphic representation of the DataSet – right-click on the **BikesDatabaseDataSet** icon in the Data Sources window and choose **Edit DataSet with Designer**.

Binding meaningful data

Having added data controls to the Form on the previous page, you can now display the data contained in the **Bikes** table, but the **ModelID** and **VersionID** fields are still displaying the ID number – not the associated value from the linked table. To correct this so the application displays meaningful data, it is necessary to bind the linked tables to those controls.

1 Click on the **Models** table icon in the **Data Sources** window, then drag it to **Form Designer** and drop it onto the **ModelID ComboBox** control – you will see **ModelsBindingSource** and **ModelsTableAdapter** items get added to the **Component Tray**

2 Click on the **Versions** table icon in the **Data Sources** window, then drag it to **Form Designer** and drop it onto the **VersionID ComboBox** control – you will see **VersionsBindingSource** and **VersionsTableAdapter** items get added to the **Component Tray**

3 Click the arrow button on each **ComboBox** control to reveal their new data binding settings on the **Smart Tag**

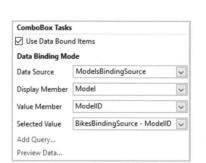

The **ModelID ComboBox** control is now bound to the **ModelsBindingSource**, so it will now display the **Model** value, rather than its ID number.

Similarly, the **VersionID ComboBox** is now bound to the **VersionsBindingSource** so it will now display the **Version** value, rather than its ID number.

4 Edit the **Label** control alongside each **ComboBox** to remove the "ID" text – reflecting the new value these controls will display

5 As the **BikeID** is not really meaningful to the user, set its **Visible** property to **False** in the **Properties** window, then delete its **Label** control

6 Run the application and see meaningful values appear

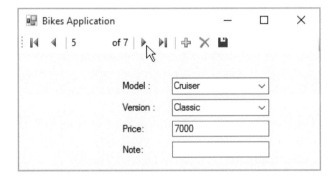

7 To test the ability to save data into the database, enter text in the **Note** field and click the **Save Data** button

8 Use the arrow buttons to move to a different item, then return to see that your text has been preserved

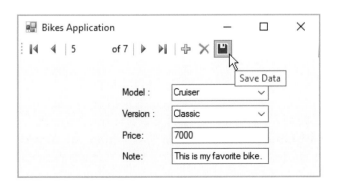

Saved data is not preserved permanently when running in Visual Studio's debug mode, but you can run **BikesApplication.exe** in the project's **bin/Debug** folder to see saved data is preserved permanently.

183

Building custom SQL queries

Having added the ability to display meaningful data on the previous page, you can now exploit the true power of databases by building custom SQL queries to extract only specific data.

 1 Select the **BikesTableAdapter** icon in the **Component Tray**, then choose **Add Query** from its **Smart Tag** options to launch the **Search Criteria Builder** dialog

Hot tip

Structured Query Language (SQL) is the standard language used to query all databases. Refer to **SQL in easy steps** to learn SQL.

The **Search Criteria Builder** dialog displays an SQL query named "FillBy", which is executed by the form's **Load** event-handler to populate the navigation **ToolStrip** and Form fields. This query selects all columns and rows of the **Bikes** table. It can be recreated as a custom SQL query that can be executed to perform the same service whenever the user requires all data to be selected.

2 Change the **New query name** field to "GetAll", then click **OK** – you will see another **ToolStrip** get added to the Form containing a button labeled **GetAll**

3 Select the new **ToolStrip**, then in the **Properties** window, set its **AutoSize** to **False** and change its **MaximumSize** and **Size** properties to resemble a single button **100, 30**

Don't forget

The Classic version is represented by the number 3, and the Cruiser model is represented by the number 2 – as shown in the table designs on page 166, and in the data entered on page 177.

To create custom SQL queries that select specific data, you can simply edit the default query by appending a qualification clause.

4 Click the **BikesTableAdapter** component icon and choose **Add Query** to open **Search Criteria Builder** again

5 Change the **New query name** field to "GetClassics", then append this code to the **Query Text** statement
WHERE VersionID = 3

Select a parameterized query to load data:

◉ New query name: `GetClassics`

○ Existing query name:

Query Text:

`SELECT BikeID, ModelID, VersionID, Price, Note FROM dbo.Bikes WHERE VersionID = 3`

6 Click **OK** to create a **ToolStrip** for this query, and resize it as before to resemble a single button

7 Reopen **Search Criteria Builder** and create a new query named "GetCruisers", appending this to the **Query Text** **WHERE ModelID = 2**

8 Resize the new **ToolStrip** as before, then run the application and click the **GetClassics** button to select data on all "Classic" versions only

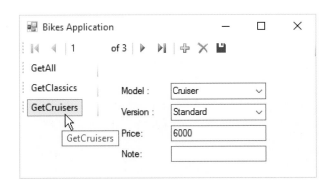

9 Click **GetAll** to select all data once more, then click **GetCruisers** to select data on all "Cruiser" models only

185

The navigation **ToolStrip** shows the number of records selected by that query – in this case two "Classic" versions and three "Cruiser" models.

Summary

- Databases store data in structured rows and columns, making it easy to reference and manipulate data.
- Each row in a database table is called a record and must have a **Primary Key** to uniquely identify that record.
- A table in a relational database can address its own records by **Primary Key** and address other tables by **Foreign Key**.
- Normalization rules insist that data must not be duplicated within a database and column data types must be defined.
- Data integrity is preserved by database constraints.
- SQL Server is integrated with Visual Studio to allow databases to be created from within the IDE.
- Table constraints are established in the **Table Definition**.
- Setting the **Primary Key** column's **Is Identity** property to **True** will automatically number each row.
- Foreign keys can be created by the **Add New Foreign Key** option of the **Foreign Keys** item in the **Table Definition**.
- New **Foreign Key** constraints must be edited to describe the parent-child relationship between two tables.
- Table constraints are tested in real-time as **Table Data** is input.
- A database **Dataset** is an in-memory representation of the data contained within the database tables.
- Drag and drop a table from the **Data Sources** window onto a Form to automatically create data controls.
- A **BindingSource** manages the data flow between a **Dataset** and Form controls.
- Drag and drop a table from the **Data Sources** window onto a control to bind meaningful data from the table to that control.
- A **TableAdapter** has methods to supply data to Form controls and can add custom SQL queries to exploit the true power of databases by selecting specific data.

Index

187

189